PRAYING WITH POPE JOHN PAUL II

PRAYING WITH
POPE JOHN PAUL II

Selected and arranged by
Paul Thigpen

HarperCollins*Publishers*

HarperCollins*Publishers* 77–85 Fulham Palace Road, London W6 8JB

First published in the USA in 1996 by Charis Books, an imprint of
Servant Publications, P.O. Box 8617, Ann Arbor, Michigan 48107

This edition first published in 1997 by HarperCollins*Publishers*

1 3 5 7 9 10 8 6 4 2

Copyright in this compilation © 1996 Paul Thigpen

A catalogue record for this book is available from the British Library

0 00 6280498

Printed and bound in Great Britain by Caledonian International Book
Manufacturing Ltd, Glasgow

CONDITIONS OF SALE

CONTENTS

LIST OF ABBREVIATIONS

INTRODUCTION

I pray with the Holy Father every morning.

That's not to say, of course, that I've ever had the high privilege of a personal audience with the Pope, much less a daily appointment for prayer at the Vatican. But for a long time now I've taken part in the old custom of "praying for the Holy Father's intentions" every day with the recitation of an Our Father, a Hail Mary, and a Glory Be. As I pray, I see him in my mind's eye, repeating the ancient words as I say them along with him, and I'm confident that our hearts are truly praying in unison—both because these three prayers must often be on his lips, and also because they no doubt sum up his intentions perfectly, just as they sum up my own.

Yet in these prayers, I've found myself wanting to know more about the specifics of "the Holy Father's intentions". What, for example, does it mean to Pope John Paul II when he calls God "Our Father"? What, concretely, is this wise and holy man asking for when he prays that God's Kingdom would come, that His will would be done on earth as it is in heaven? What needs of humankind does he focus on when he asks for "our daily bread"; what particular sins of the Church and of the world does he confess when he begs the Father to "forgive us our trespasses"?

At least a partial answer to these questions can be found in the prayers collected within this little volume and accompanied by passages from Scripture that provide them a context. In these joyful praises, urgent petitions, and profound meditations, we hear the heartbeat of Pope John Paul II. We have the fascinating and humbling opportunity to listen in while he pours out his soul to God and to the saints who reign with God; and in his words we find laid bare the joys and griefs, the fears and hopes, that shape his life and his mission.

"More things are wrought by prayer / Than this world dreams of," said Tennyson. "For so the whole round earth is every way / Bound by gold chains about the feet of God." The Holy Father maintains what may be the world's most daunting and exhausting schedule, yet by all accounts of those closest to him he somehow manages to hammer out many such "gold chains" throughout every day. As he prays, he struggles mightily to pull the world back home from its prodigal wanderings and to secure it lovingly to the feet of God the Father.

Here is a little treasure chest of some golden links of prayer Pope John Paul II has forged over the years. In them, he invites us to join him in binding earth to heaven. Today, as the world wanders far from God in confusion and despair, it dreams of peace, of justice, of happiness and fulfilment—thus dreaming, unawares, of the coming of God's Kingdom. Can we dare to believe that the Holy Father's prayers, multiplied by our own, might one day accomplish, as Tennyson said, even more than all the world has dreamed of?

Such a hope—such a challenge—should drive us all to our knees to take our place praying alongside this devoted "servant of the servants of God".

Paul Thigpen, All Saints' Day, 1995

MEDITATIONS ON PRAYER
BY POPE JOHN PAUL II

PRAYER, THE CENTRE OF OUR LIVES
Truly Christian prayer ... leads to sharing in the Son's own
filial dialogue with the Father in accordance with Saint Paul's
marvellous expression in the Letter to the Galatians: "Because
you are sons, God has sent the Spirit of His Son into our
hearts, crying, 'Abba! Father!'"[1] Prayer is not one occupation
among many, but is at the centre of our life in Christ. It turns
our attention away from ourselves and directs it to the Lord.
Prayer fills the mind with truth and gives hope to the heart.
Without a deep experience of prayer, growth in the moral life
will be shallow. [TPS 39/2, 1994, 115-6]

PRAYER, AS ESSENTIAL AS BREATHING
"Lord, teach us to pray."[2] When, on the slopes of the
Mount of Olives, the apostles addressed Jesus with these
words, they were not asking an ordinary question, but with
spontaneous trust, they were expressing one of the deepest
needs of the human heart.

To tell the truth, today's world does not make much room for that need. The hectic pace of daily activity, combined with the noisy and often frivolous invasiveness of the means of communication, is certainly not something conducive to the interior recollection required for prayer. Then, too, there are deeper difficulties: modern people have an increasingly less religious view of the world and life. The secularization process seems to have persuaded them that the course of events can be sufficiently explained by the interplay of this world's immanent forces, independent of higher intervention. The achievements of science and technology have also fostered their conviction that they already have, and will continue to increase, their ability to dominate situations, directing them according to their own desires.

In Christian circles, too, there is a widespread "functional" view of prayer which threatens to compromise its transcendent nature. Some claim that one truly finds God by being open to one's neighbour. Therefore, prayer would not mean being removed from the world's distractions in order to be recollected in conversation with God. It would rather be expressed in an unconditional commitment to charity for others. Authentic prayer, therefore, would be the works of charity, and they alone.

In reality, [however,] because they are creatures in and of themselves incomplete and needy, human beings spontaneously turn to Him who is the source of every gift, in order to praise Him, make intercession, and in Him seek to fulfil the tormenting desire which inflames their hearts. Saint Augustine understood this quite well when he noted:

"You have made us for Yourself, O Lord, and our hearts are restless until they rest in You."[3]

For this very reason the experience of prayer, as a basic act of the believer, is common to all religions, including those in which there is only a rather vague belief in a personal God or in which it is confused by false representations.

Prayer particularly belongs to the Christian religion, in which it occupies a central position. Jesus urges us to "pray always without becoming weary".[4] Christians know that for them prayer is as essential as breathing, and once they have tasted the sweetness of intimate conversation with God, they do not hesitate to immerse themselves in it with trusting abandonment.   [TPS 38/1, 1993, 44-5]

THE "CONTEMPLATIVE OUTLOOK"

We need ... to foster, in ourselves and in others, a contemplative outlook. Such an outlook arises from faith in the God of life, who has created every individual as a wonder.[5] It is the outlook of those who see life in its deeper meaning, who grasp its utter gratuitousness, its beauty and its invitation to freedom and responsibility. It is the outlook of those who do not presume to take possession of reality but instead accept it as a gift, discovering in all things the reflection of the Creator and seeing in every person His living image.[6]

This outlook does not give in to discouragement when confronted by those who are sick, suffering, outcast, or at death's door. Instead, in all these situations it feels challenged to find meaning, and precisely in the face of every person [it finds] a call to encounter, dialogue, and solidarity.

It is time for all of us to adopt this outlook, and with deep religious awe to rediscover the ability to revere and honour every person … Inspired by this contemplative outlook, the new people of the redeemed cannot but respond with songs of joy, praise, and thanksgiving for the priceless gift of life, for the mystery of every individual's call to share through Christ in the life of grace and in an existence of unending communion with God our Creator and Father.　　　[EV n. 83]

PRAYER MUST BE UNITED TO ACTION

All of you, through the different forms of spirituality by which you are inspired and which constitute a rich spiritual heritage for the Church and humanity, are trying to live a really Christian and evangelical life, as laity and as Christians "in the world" without being "of the world".[7] For you lay people, this apostolic life calls for effective openness to your various environments in order to cause the evangelical "leaven" to penetrate them. It involves multiple activities and responsibilities to be assumed in all areas of human life: the family, professions, society, culture, and politics. It is by assuming these responsibilities competently and in deep union with God that you will fulfil your vocation as laity and Christians: that you will sanctify yourselves and sanctify the world.

To remain united with God in the accomplishment of the tasks incumbent upon you is a vital necessity to bear witness to His Love. Only a sacramental life and a life of prayer will be able to cause this intimacy with the Lord to grow.

To take time to pray, and to nourish prayer and activities through biblical, theological, and doctrinal study; to live by

Christ and His grace by receiving assiduously the Sacraments of Reconciliation and the Eucharist—such are the fundamental requirements of every deeply Christian life. Thus the Holy Spirit will be the source both of your action and of your contemplation, which will then interpenetrate each other, support each other, and yield abundant fruit.

This deep unity between prayer and action is at the basis of all spiritual renewal, especially among the laity. It is at the basis of the great enterprises of evangelization and construction of the world according to God's plan. [OR 5-5-80, 5]

THE HOLY SPIRIT AND PRAYER

The breath of the divine life, the Holy Spirit, in its simplest and most common manner, expresses itself and makes itself felt in prayer. It is a beautiful and salutary thought that, wherever people are praying in the world, there the Holy Spirit is, the living breath of prayer. It is a beautiful and salutary thought to recognize that—if prayer is offered throughout the world, in the past, in the present, and in the future—equally widespread is the presence and action of the Holy Spirit, who "breathes" prayer in the heart of man in all the endless range of the most varied situations and conditions, [which are] sometimes favourable and sometimes unfavourable to the spiritual and religious life.

Many times, through the influence of the Spirit, prayer rises from the human heart in spite of prohibitions and persecutions and even official proclamations regarding the nonreligious or even atheistic character of public life. Prayer always remains the voice of all those who apparently have no voice—and in this voice there always echoes that "loud cry" attributed to Christ by the Letter to the Hebrews.[8]

Prayer is also the revelation of that abyss which is the heart of man: a depth which comes from God and which only God can fill, precisely with the Holy Spirit. We read in Luke: "If you, then, who are evil, know how to give good gifts to your children, how much more will the heavenly Father give the Holy Spirit to those who ask him!"[9]

The Holy Spirit is the Gift that comes into man's heart together with prayer. In prayer He manifests Himself first of all and above all as the Gift that "helps us in our weakness". This is the magnificent thought developed by Saint Paul in the Letter to the Romans, when he writes: "For we do not know how to pray as we ought, but the Spirit Himself intercedes for us with sighs too deep for words."[10]

Therefore, the Holy Spirit not only enables us to pray, but guides us from within in prayer: He is present in our prayer and gives it a divine dimension. Thus "He who searches the hearts of men knows what is the mind of the Spirit, because the Spirit intercedes for the saints according to the will of God."[11] Prayer through the power of the Holy Spirit becomes the ever more mature expression of the new man, who by means of this prayer participates in the divine life. [DV n. 65]

THE GIFT OF THE SPIRIT INCLUDES
THE ANSWER TO EVERY PRAYER

"Our Father, who art in heaven ..."[12]

According to [these words]—Christ's answer to the request "teach us to pray"—everything is reduced to this single concept: to learn to pray means "to learn the Father". If we learn the Father reality in the full sense of the word, in its full dimension, we have learned everything. To learn the Father means finding the answer to ... questions that ... arise from the fact that I pray and in some cases my prayer is not granted ...

To learn who the Father is means learning what absolute trust is. To learn the Father means acquiring the certainty that ... He does not refuse you even when everything—materially and psychologically—seems to indicate refusal. He never refuses you.

So learning to pray means "learning the Father" in this way: learning to be sure that the Father never refuses you anything, but that on the contrary, He gives the Holy Spirit to those who ask Him.[13]

The gifts we ask for are various; they are our necessities. We ask according to our needs and it cannot be otherwise. Christ confirms this attitude of ours: Yes, it is so; you must ask according to your needs, as you feel them ... [Nevertheless, you must recognize that] the answer to every request of yours... is always given through a substantial Gift: the Father gives us the Holy Spirit ...

Learning to pray means learning the Father and learning absolute trust in Him who always offers us this greatest Gift. And in offering it He never deceives us. If sometimes, or even often, we do not directly receive what we ask for, [yet] in this so great Gift—when it is offered to us—all other gifts are contained, even if we do not always realize this.

[OR 9-1-80, 5]

THE PRAYER OF THE SAINTS

The mission of reconciliation is proper to the whole Church, also and especially to that Church which has already been admitted to the full sharing in divine glory with the Virgin Mary—the angels and the saints, who contemplate and adore the thrice-holy God. The Church in heaven, the Church on earth, and the Church in purgatory are mysteriously united in this co-operation with Christ in reconciling the world to God.

The first means of this [saving] action is that of prayer. It is certain that the Blessed Virgin, Mother of Christ and of the Church, and the saints, who have now reached the end of their earthly journey and possess God's glory, sustain by their intercession their brethren who are on pilgrimage through the world, in the commitment to conversion, to faith, to getting up again after every fall, to acting in order to help the growth of communion and peace in the Church and in the world. In the mystery of the communion of saints, universal reconciliation is accomplished in its most profound form, which is also the most fruitful for the salvation of all.

[RP n. 12]

FAMILY PRAYER

The Church prays for the Christian family and educates the family to live in generous accord with the priestly gift and role received from Christ the high priest. In effect, the baptismal priesthood of the faithful exercised in the sacrament of Matrimony constitutes the basis of a priestly vocation and mission for the spouses and family by which their daily lives are transformed into "spiritual sacrifices acceptable to God through Jesus Christ".[14] This transformation is achieved not only by celebrating the Eucharist and the other sacraments and through offering themselves to the glory of God, but also through a life of prayer, through prayerful dialogue with the Father, through Jesus Christ, in the Holy Spirit.

Family prayer has its own characteristic qualities. It is prayer offered in common, husband and wife together, parents and children together. Communion in prayer is both a consequence of and a requirement for the communion bestowed by the Sacraments of Baptism and Matrimony. The words with which the Lord Jesus promises His presence can be applied to the members of the Christian family in a special way: "Again I say to you, if two of you agree on earth about anything they ask, it will be done for them by my Father in heaven. For where two or three are gathered in my name, there am I in the midst of them."[15]

Family prayer has for its very own object family life itself, which in all its varying circumstances is seen as a call from God and lived as a filial response to His call. Joys and sorrows, hopes and disappointments, births and birthday celebrations, wedding anniversaries of the parents, departures, separations and homecomings, important and far-reaching decisions, the death of those who are dear … all of these mark God's loving intervention in the family's history. They should be seen as suitable moments for thanksgiving, for petition, for trusting abandonment of the family into the hands of their common Father in heaven. The dignity and responsibility of the Christian family as the domestic church can be achieved only with God's unceasing aid, which will surely be granted if it is humbly and trustingly petitioned in prayer.

By reason of their dignity and mission, Christian parents have the specific responsibility of educating their children in prayer, introducing them to gradual discovery of the mystery of God and to personal dialogue with Him … The concrete example and living witness of parents is fundamental and irreplaceable in educating their children to pray. Only by praying together with their children can a father and mother—exercising their royal priesthood—penetrate the innermost depths of their children's hearts and leave an impression that the future events in their lives will not be able to efface. [FC n. 59, 60]

PRAYER IS ESSENTIAL FOR PEACE

I wish to reaffirm the need for intense, humble, confident, and persevering prayer, if the world is finally to become a dwelling-place of peace.

Prayer is *par excellence* the power needed to implore that peace and obtain it. It gives courage and support to all who love this good and desire to promote it in accordance with their own possibilities and in the various situations in which they live.

Prayer not only opens us up to a meeting with the Most High but also disposes us to a meeting with our neighbour, helping us to establish with everyone, without discrimination, relationships of respect, understanding, esteem, and love ...

Prayer is the bond which most effectively unites us. It is through prayer that believers meet one another at a level where inequalities, misunderstandings, bitterness, and hostility are overcome, namely before God, the Lord and Father of all. Prayer, as the authentic expression of a right relationship with God and with others, is already a positive contribution to peace. [TPS 37/3, 1992, 161-3, 166]

RENEWAL OF PRAYER IS A SIGN OF HOPE

Our difficult age has a special need of prayer. In the course of history—both in the past and in the present—many men and women have borne witness to the importance of prayer by consecrating themselves to the praise of God and to the life of prayer, especially in monasteries and convents. So, too, recent years have been seeing a growth in the number of people who, in ever more widespread movements and groups, are giving first place to prayer and seeking in prayer a renewal of their spiritual life. This is a significant and comforting sign, for from this experience there is coming a real contribution to the revival of prayer among the faithful, who have been helped to gain a clearer idea of the Holy Spirit as He who inspires in hearts a profound yearning for holiness.

In many individuals and many communities there is a growing awareness that, even with all the rapid progress of technological and scientific civilization, and despite the real conquests and goals attained, man is threatened, humanity is threatened. In the face of this danger, and indeed already experiencing the frightful reality of man's spiritual decadence, individuals and whole communities, guided as it were by an inner sense of faith, are seeking the strength to raise man up again, to save him from himself, from his own errors and mistakes that often make harmful his very conquests. And thus they are discovering prayer, in which the "Spirit [who] helps us in our weakness"[16] manifests Himself. In this way the times in which we are living are bringing the Holy Spirit closer to the many who are returning to prayer.   [DV n. 65]

PRAYER, A CATEGORICAL IMPERATIVE
We hear within us, as a resounding echo, the words that [Christ] spoke: "Apart from me you can do nothing."[17] We feel not only the need but even a categorical imperative for great, intense, and growing prayer by all the Church. Only prayer can prevent all [our] great succeeding tasks and difficulties from becoming a source of crisis and make them instead the occasion and, as it were, the foundation for ever more mature achievements on the People of God's march towards the Promised Land in this stage of history approaching the end of the second millennium.

Accordingly, … with a warm and humble call to prayer, I wish the Church to devote herself to this prayer, together with Mary the Mother of Jesus, as the apostles and disciples of the Lord did in the Upper Room in Jerusalem after His ascension.[18] Above all, I implore Mary, the heavenly Mother of the Church, to be so good as to devote herself to this prayer of humanity's new advent, together with us who make up the Church, that is to say the Mystical Body of her only Son. I hope that through this prayer we shall be able to receive the Holy Spirit coming upon us and thus become Christ's witnesses "to the end of the earth",[19] like those who went forth from the Upper Room in Jerusalem on the day of Pentecost.   [RH n. 22]

But Jesus called them to Him and said, "You know that the rulers of the Gentiles lord it over them, and their great men exercise authority over them. It shall not be so among you; but whoever would be great among you must be your servant, and whoever would be first among you must be your slave; even as the Son of man came not to be served but to serve, and to give His life as a ransom for many."
MATTHEW 20:25-28

A PRAYER OF JOHN PAUL II
AT THE BEGINNING OF HIS PONTIFICATE

The new successor of Peter in the see of Rome, today makes a fervent, humble, and trusting prayer: Christ, make me become and remain the servant of Your unique power, the servant of Your sweet power, the servant of Your power that knows no eventide. Make me be a servant. Indeed, the servant of Your servants. [OR 11-2-78]

PRAYERS TO GOD THE FATHER

For this reason I bow my knees before the Father, from whom every family in heaven and on earth is named, that according to the riches of His glory He may grant you to be strengthened with might through His Spirit in the inner man, and that Christ may dwell in your hearts through faith...

EPHESIANS 3:14-17

TO GOD FOR GUIDANCE

With all my heart I seek You;
let me not stray from Your commands . . .
Open my eyes, that I may consider
the wonders of Your law.
I am a wayfarer of earth;
hide not Your commands from me . . .
Make me understand the way of Your precepts,
and I will meditate on Your wondrous deeds . . .
Your compassion is great, O Lord . . .

PSALM 119:10, 18-19, 27, 156 NAB

O God, You are our Creator.
You are good and Your mercy knows no bounds.
To You arises the praise of every creature.
O God, You have given us an inner law by which we must
   live.

To do Your will is our task.

To follow Your ways is to know peace of heart.

To You we offer our homage.

Guide us on all the paths we travel upon this earth.

Free us from all the evil tendencies which lead our hearts
away from Your will.

Never allow us to stray from You.

O God, judge of all humankind, help us to be included
among Your chosen ones on the last day.

O God, Author of peace and justice, give us true joy and
authentic love, and a lasting solidarity among peoples.

Give us Your everlasting gifts. Amen!

May the God of mercy, the God of love, the God of peace
bless each of you and all the members of your families!

[TPS 37/4, 1992, 213]

FOR GOD'S MERCY

For we ourselves were once foolish, disobedient, led astray, slaves to various passions and pleasures, passing our days in malice and envy, hated by men and hating one another; but when the goodness and loving kindness of God our Saviour appeared, He saved us, not because of deeds done by us in righteousness, but in virtue of His own mercy, by the washing of regeneration and renewal in the Holy Spirit, which He poured out upon us richly through Jesus Christ our Saviour, so that we might be justified by His grace and become heirs in hope of eternal life.

TITUS 3:3-7

In the name of Jesus Christ crucified and risen, in the spirit of His messianic mission, enduring in the history of humanity, we raise our voices and pray that the Love which is in the Father may once again be revealed at this stage in history, and that, through the work of the Son and the Holy Spirit, it may be shown to be present in our modern world and to be more powerful than sin and death. We pray for this through the intercession of her who does not cease to proclaim "mercy ... from generation to generation",[1] and also through the intercession of those for whom there have been completely fulfilled the words of the Sermon on the Mount: "Blessed are the merciful, for they shall obtain mercy."[2]

[DM n. 15]

WITH CHRIST TO THE FATHER

For in Him all the fullness of God was pleased to dwell, and through Him to reconcile to Himself all things, whether on earth or in heaven, making peace by the blood of His cross.

COLOSSIANS 1:19-20

Let us cry out and pray with Christ:

"Father, forgive them; for they know not what they do."[3]

"My God, my God, why hast Thou forsaken Me?"[4]

"Father, into Thy hands I commit My Spirit."[5]

Let us cry out and pray as though echoing these words of Christ:

Father, accept us all in the cross of Christ; accept the Church and humanity, the Church and the world.

Accept those who accept the cross; those who do not understand it and those who avoid it; those who do not accept it; and those who fight it in order to erase and

6

uproot this sign from the land of the living.

Father, accept us all in the cross of Your Son!

Accept each of us in the cross of Christ!

Disregarding everything that happens in man's heart, disregarding the fruits of his works and of the events of the modern world, accept man!

May the cross of Your Son remain as the sign of the acceptance of the prodigal son by the Father.

May it remain as the sign of the Covenant, of the new and eternal Covenant.   [OR 4-14-80, 4]

LISTEN TO US!

O Shepherd of Israel, hearken,
O guide of the flock of Joseph!
From Your throne upon the cherubim, shine forth...
Rouse Your power,
and come to save us!
O Lord of hosts, restore us;
if Your face shine upon us,
then we shall be safe.

PSALM 80:1-3 NAB

Listen to us, O Lord!

In the spirit of Christ, our Lord, let us pray for the Catholic Church, for the other Churches, for the whole of mankind.

Listen to us, Lord!

Let us pray for all those who suffer persecution for the sake of justice and for those who are striving for freedom and peace.

Listen to us, Lord!

Let us pray for those who exercise a ministry in the Church, for those who have special responsibilities in social life, and for all those who are in the service of the little and the weak.

Listen to us, Lord!

Let us ask God for ourselves for the courage to persevere in our commitment for the realization of the unity of all Christians.

Listen to us, Lord!

Lord God, we trust in You. Grant that we may act in a way that is pleasing to You. Grant that we may be faithful servants of Your glory. Amen.   [OR 1-22-79, 12]

TO A MERCIFUL GOD,
PRAYING WITH JEWS AND MUSLIMS

*Be merciful,
even as your Father is merciful.*

LUKE 6:36

Within me is the deep conviction that the merciful God wishes to see this characteristic [of mercy] more clearly reflected in the entire human family: authentic mercy seems to me something which is indispensable to giving shape and solidity to relations among men, inspired by the deepest respect for all that is human and for brotherhood.

In effect, Christians are exhorted to imitate the Lord Jesus, model of mercy. Judaism also considers mercy a fundamental commandment ... Islam, in its profession of faith, attributes this trait to God. And Abraham, our common ancestor, teaches everyone—Christians, Jews, and Muslims—to follow this way of mercy and of love ...

[So I lift] up my spirit in a prayer to the merciful God:

— O Ineffable One, of whom all creation speaks;
— O Almighty One, who never forces, but only invites and
   guides mankind towards good;
— O Compassionate One, who desires mercy among all men:
   May He always guide us along His paths, fill our hearts
with His love, with His peace and joy, and bless us!

[OR 6-28-82, 16]

PRAYERS TO GOD THE SON

Since then we have a great high priest who has passed through the heavens, Jesus, the Son of God, let us hold fast our confession. For we have not a high priest who is unable to sympathize with our weaknesses, but one who in every respect has been tempted as we are, yet without sinning. Let us then with confidence draw near to the throne of grace, that we may receive mercy and find grace to help in time of need.

HEBREWS 4:14-16

HYMN TO CHRIST

*God is faithful, by whom you were
called into the fellowship of His
Son, Jesus Christ our Lord.*

1 CORINTHIANS 1:9

Christ of our sufferings,
Christ of our sacrifices,
Christ of our Gethsemane,
Christ of our difficult transformations,
Christ of our faithful service to our neighbour,
Christ of our pilgrimage...
Christ of our community...
Christ our Redeemer,
Christ our Brother!
Amen.   [OR 2-26-79, 5]

BENEATH THE CROSS OF CHRIST

For the word of the cross is folly to those who are perishing, but to us who are being saved, it is the power of God... We preach Christ crucified,... Christ the power of God and the wisdom of God. For the foolishness of God is wiser than men, and the weakness of God is stronger than men.

1 CORINTHIANS 1:18, 23-25

And behold: we who ... are standing ... beneath the cross of the ages, wish, through Your cross and passion, O Christ, *to cry out today* that mercy [which] has irreversibly entered into the history of man, into our whole human history—and which in spite of the appearances of weakness is stronger than evil. It is the greatest power and force upon which man can sustain himself, threatened as he is from so many sides ...

Holy is God.

Holy and strong.

Holy immortal One, have mercy on us.

Have mercy: *eleison: misere.*

May the power of Your love once more be shown to be greater than the evil that threatens it. May it be shown to be *greater than sin* ...

May the power of Your cross, O Christ, be shown to be *greater than the author of sin,* who is called "the prince of this world".[1]

For by Your blood and Your passion You have *redeemed the world!*   [OR 4-27-81, 8]

TO THE RESURRECTED CHRIST

I have been crucified with Christ; it is no longer I who live, but Christ who lives in me; and the life I now live in the flesh I live by faith in the Son of God, who loved me and gave Himself for me.

GALATIANS 2:20

Your resurrection, Christ, is the glory of the Father.

Your resurrection reveals the glory of the Father, to whom, at the moment of death, You entrusted Yourself up to the end, committing Your spirit with the following words: "Father, into Thy hands."[2] And together with Yourself, You entrusted all of us, dying on the cross as the Son of Man: our Brother and Redeemer. In Your death You gave back to the Father our human death, You gave back the being of every man, which is marked by death.

Lo, the Father gives back to You, Son of Man, this life that You had entrusted to Him up to the end. You rise from the dead thanks to the glory of the Father. The Father

17

is glorified in the resurrection, and You are glorified in the Father, to whom You entrusted Your life in death up to the end: You are glorified with life. With new life. With the identical and, at the same time, new life.

You are the Christ, the Son of the living God, whom the Father glorified with resurrection and life in the midst of man's history. In Your death, You restored to the Father the being of each of us, the life of every man, which is marked by the necessity of death, in order that in Your resurrection each one could acquire again the consciousness and the certainty of entering the new life, through You and together with You.

"For if we have been united with Him in a death like His, we shall certainly be united with Him in a resurrection like His ..."[3]

Christ, the Son of the living God ... give us the joy of that new life, which we bear within us, which only You can give to the human heart:

You, the risen Christ!   [OR 4-14-80, 4, 12]

THANKSGIVING FOR THE EUCHARIST

For our paschal lamb, Christ, has been sacrificed. Therefore let us celebrate the feast!

1 CORINTHIANS 5:7-8 NAB

O Christ the Saviour, we give You thanks for Your redeeming sacrifice, the only hope of men!

O Christ the Saviour, we give You thanks for the eucharistic breaking of bread, which You instituted in order to really meet Your brothers, in the course of the centuries!

O Christ the Saviour, put into the hearts of the baptized the desire to offer themselves with You and to commit themselves for the salvation of their brothers!

You who are really present in the Blessed Sacrament, spread Your blessings abundantly on Your people ... Amen. [OR 7-27-81, 2]

TO CHRIST IN THE BLESSED SACRAMENT

Jesus said to them, "I am the bread of life; he who comes to me shall not hunger, and he who believes in me shall never thirst … Truly, truly, I say to you, unless you eat the flesh of the Son of man and drink His blood, you have no life in you … For my flesh is food indeed, and my blood is drink indeed. He who eats my flesh and drinks my blood abides in me, and I in him."

JOHN 6:35, 53, 55-56

"Lord, stay with us."

These words were spoken for the first time by the disciples of Emmaus.[4] Subsequently in the course of the centuries they have been spoken, an infinite number of times, by the lips of so many of Your disciples and confessors, O Christ …

I speak the same words today. I speak them to invite You, Christ, in Your eucharistic presence, to accept the

20

daily adoration continuing through the entire day, in this temple, in this basilica, in this chapel.

Stay with us and stay, from now on, every day, according to the desire of my heart ...

Stay! That we may meet You in the prayer of adoration and thanksgiving, in the prayer of expiation and petition, to which all those who visit this basilica are invited.

Stay! You who are at one and the same time veiled in the eucharistic mystery of faith and are also revealed under the species of bread and wine, which You have assumed in this sacrament.

Stay! That Your presence in this temple may be incessantly reconfirmed, and that all those who enter here may become aware that it is Your house, "the dwelling of God ...with men",[5] and, visiting this basilica, may find in it the very source of life and holiness that gushes from Your eucharistic heart.   [OR 12-14-81, 10-11]

TO THE MERCIFUL LOVE OF THE CRUCIFIED KING

Blessed be the God and Father of our Lord Jesus Christ! By His great mercy we have been born anew to a living hope through the resurrection of Jesus Christ from the dead, and to an inheritance which is imperishable, undefiled, and unfading, kept in heaven for you, who by God's power are guarded through faith for a salvation ready to be revealed in the last time.

1 PETER 1:3-5

Merciful Love, we pray to You, do not fail!
Merciful Love, be tireless!
Be constantly greater than every evil which is in man and in the world. Be greater than that evil which has increased in our century and in our generation!
Be more powerful with the power of the crucified King!
"Blessed be His Kingdom which is coming."

[OR 4-30-79, 7]

TO RENEW THE FACE OF THE EARTH

*For I will pour water on the thirsty land, and
streams on the dry ground;
I will pour My Spirit upon your descendants, and
My blessing on your offspring.*

ISAIAH 44:3

"O most blessed Light divine,
Shine within these hearts of Yours,
And our inmost being fill!"[1]
Fill these hearts in our times, in which the face of the
earth has been so enriched thanks to man's creativity and
labour through the works of science and technology, when
there has been so profound an exploration of the interior of
the earth and of the spaces of the universe, and when at the
same time mankind finds itself face-to-face with previous[ly]
unknown menaces from forces that man himself has released.

Today, we, the pastors of the Church, heirs of those
who received the Holy Spirit in the Upper Room of
Pentecost, must go forth as they did, conscious of the

immensity of the Gift that is given in the Church to the human family. We must go forth, continually go forth into the world and, in the different places on earth where we are, we must repeat with still greater fervour:

"Let Your Spirit descend and renew the face of the earth."

Let Him descend.

Throughout the history of mankind, throughout the history of the visible world, the Church does not cease to confess:

"We believe in the Spirit."

"We believe in the Holy Spirit, the Lord, the Giver of life."

"Credo in Spiritum Sanctum, Dominum et vivicantem."

In this Spirit we remain. Amen.   [OR 6-15-81, 6]

FOR THR RIGHTEOUSNESS,
PEACE, AND JOY OF THE SPIRIT

Do not grieve the Holy Spirit of God, in whom you were sealed for the day of redemption. Let all bitterness and wrath and anger and clamour and slander be put away from you, with all malice, and be kind to one another, tender-hearted, forgiving one another, as God in Christ forgave you.

EPHESIANS 4:30-32

The Church with her heart which embraces all human hearts implores from the Holy Spirit that happiness which only in God has its complete realization: the joy "that no one will be able to take away",[2] the joy which is the fruit of love, and therefore of God who is love; she implores "the righteousness, the peace, and the joy of the Holy Spirit" in which, in the words of Saint Paul, consists the Kingdom of God.[3]

Peace too is the fruit of love: that interior peace, which weary man seeks in his inmost being; that peace besought by humanity, the human family, peoples, nations, continents, anxiously hoping to obtain it in the prospect of the transition from the second to the third Christian millennium. Since the way of peace passes in the last analysis through love and seeks to create the civilization of love, the Church fixes her eyes on Him who is the love of the Father and the Son, and in spite of increasing dangers she does not cease to trust, she does not cease to invoke and to serve the peace of man on earth. Her trust is based on Him who, being the Spirit-love, is also the Spirit of peace and does not cease to be present in our human world, on the horizon of minds and hearts, in order to fill the universe with love and peace.

Before Him I kneel … and implore Him, as the Spirit of the Father and the Son, to grant to all of us the blessing and grace which I desire to pass on, in the name of the Most Holy Trinity, to the sons and daughters of the Church and to the whole human family.   [DV n. 67]

TO AVOID GRIEVING THE SPIRIT

May [the] Counsellor—the "Spirit of truth"[4]—be
with us through His holy gifts! May there be with us
wisdom and understanding, knowledge and counsel,
fortitude, piety, and the holy fear of God,[5] so that we
may always know how to discern what comes from You
and to distinguish what comes from the "spirit of the
world", or even from the "ruler of this world".[6]

Save us from *"grieving Your Spirit"*:[7]

— by our lack of faith and lack of readiness to witness
to Your Gospel "in deed and in truth";[8]

— by secularism and by wishing at all costs to conform
to the mentality of this world;[9]

— by a lack of that love which is "patient and kind",
which "is not boastful" and which "does not insist
on its own way", which "bears all things, believes
all things, hopes all things, endures all things"—
that love which "rejoices in the right" and only in
the right.[10]

Save us from grieving Your Spirit:

— by everything that brings inward sadness and is an
obstacle for the soul;

— by whatever causes ... divisions;
— by whatever makes us a fertile soil for all temptations.

[OR 4-5,12-82, 3]

IV

PRAYERS FOR THE CHURCH

The Lord is the strength of His people,
the saving refuge of His anointed.
Save Your people, and bless Your inheritance;
feed them, and carry them forever!

PSALM 28:8-9 NAB

"THAT THEY MAY ALL BE ONE"

" I pray not only for them, but also for those who will believe in me through their word, so that they may all be one, as You, Father, are in Me and I in You, that they also may be in Us, that the world may believe that You sent Me."

JOHN 17:20-21 NAB

Let us … raise our prayer, and say together: *"That they may all be one."*[1]

That, straight away, Christians may bear common witness to the service of His kingdom. Let us pray!

All: That they may all be one.

That all Christian communities may unite in the pursuit of full unity. Let us pray!

All: That they may all be one.

That the perfect unity of all Christians may be realized so that God may be glorified by all men in Christ the Lord. Let us pray!

All: That they may all be one.

That all peoples on earth may overcome conflicts and self-ishness and find full reconciliation and peace in the Kingdom of God. Let us pray!

All: That they may all be one.

Let us pray: Remember Your Church, O Lord: preserve her from all evil: make her perfect in Your love; sanctify her and gather her from the four winds into Your Kingdom, which You have prepared for her. For Yours is the power and the glory for ever and ever.[2]

All: Amen.   [OR 1-28-80, 12]

FOR THE GIFT OF CHRISTIAN UNITY

*O nly let your manner of life be worthy of the
gospel, so that . . . you may stand firm in one
spirit, with one mind striving side by side for the
faith of the gospel . . . So if there is any encouragement in Christ, any incentive of love, any
participation in the Spirit, any affection and
sympathy, complete my joy by being of the same
mind, having the same love, being in full accord
and of one mind.*

PHILIPPIANS 1:27, 2:1-2

Let us ask the Lord to strengthen in all Christians faith in
Christ, the Saviour of the world.

All: Listen to us, O Lord.

Let us ask the Lord to sustain and guide Christians with
His gifts along the way to full unity.

All: Listen to us, O Lord.

Let us ask the Lord for the gift of unity and peace for the world.

All: Listen to us, O Lord.

Let us pray: We ask You, O Lord, for the gifts of Your Spirit. Enable us to penetrate the depth of the whole truth, and grant that we may share with others the goods that You put at our disposal.

Teach us to overcome divisions. Send us Your Spirit to lead to full unity Your sons and daughters in full charity, in obedience to Your will, through Christ our Lord. Amen.

[OR 1-26-81]

FOR FULL COMMUNION AMONG CHRISTIANS

I therefore, a prisoner for the Lord, beg you to lead a life worthy of the calling to which you have been called, with all lowliness and meekness, with patience, forbearing one another in love, eager to maintain the unity of the Spirit in the bond of peace. There is one body and one Spirit, just as you were called to the one hope that belongs to your call, one Lord, one faith, one baptism, one God and Father of us all, who is above all and through all and in all.

EPHESIANS 4:1-6

Prayer is the most important thing of all: a prayer which is ever more intense than we have raised up to God until now, a communal prayer which places us *together* in Christ's presence. Though we are divided, the Christ in whom we believe, the Christ to whom we pray together, is one and undivided. When we pray together in His name, He is in our midst,[3] to say to the Father: *"Ut omnes unum sint"* ["That they may all be one"].[4]

Christ's prayer is superior to any prayer we could make, to anything to which we could testify. With the strength we receive from Him we could attempt the impossible—"For human beings it is impossible, but not with God!"[5]—in order to re-establish that unity among Christians which for centuries was the inheritance of those who believe in Christ ...

Let us pray that the Father's will may be done, making all people children of God through the unifying action of the Spirit. Let us pray that, with full communion re-established, Christians can proclaim together: "Behold our God ... Let us rejoice and be glad that He has saved us!"[6] Amen!

[TPS 37/3, 1992, 184-5]

A LITANY FOR UNITY

*B*ehold, how good and pleasant it is
when brothers dwell in unity!...
For there the Lord has commanded the blessing,
Life for evermore.

PSALM 133:1, 3

For all the baptized, that they may proclaim Thy Kingdom to all people with their lives, let us pray:

All: May all find their dwelling in Thee, O Lord.

For Christian families, that they may bear witness of love and unity, let us pray:

All: May all find their dwelling in Thee, O Lord.

For our Christian communities, that they may be for all a dwelling of brotherhood, let us pray:

All: May all find their dwelling in Thee, O Lord.

For Christians scattered throughout the world, that they may be one, let us pray:

All: May all find their dwelling in Thee, O Lord.

For all men, that they may find reconciliation and peace in Thy Church, let us pray:

All: May all find their dwelling in Thee, O Lord.

Let us pray: "Lord, our God, save Thy people, and bless Thy heritage; keep the whole of Thy Church in peace; sanctify those who love Thy dwelling. You, in return, glorify them with Thy power and do not abandon us who hope in Thee."[7] Amen.   [OR 1-25-82, 7]

FOR UNITY AMONG THE BISHOPS

Now the company of those who believed were of one heart and soul, and no one said that any of the things which he possessed was his own, but they had everything in common. And with great power the apostles gave their testimony to the resurrection of the Lord Jesus, and great grace was upon them all.

ACTS 4:32-33

We are all equally indebted to our Redeemer. We should all listen together to that Spirit of truth and of love whom He has promised to the Church and who is operative within her. In the name of this truth and of this love, in the name of the crucified Christ and of His Mother, I ask you, and beg you: Let us abandon all opposition and division, and let us all unite in this great mission of salvation which is the price and at the same time the fruit of our redemption. The Apostolic See will continue to do all that

40

is possible to provide the means of ensuring that unity of which we speak. Let everyone avoid anything in his own way of acting which could "grieve the Holy Spirit".[8]

In order that this unity and the constant and systematic collaboration which leads to it may be perseveringly continued, I beg on my knees that, through the intercession of Mary, holy spouse of the Holy Spirit and Mother of the Church, we may all receive the light of the Holy Spirit.

[DC n. 13]

TO THE MOTHER OF PRIESTS

*"Her priests I will clothe with salvation,
and her saints will shout for joy."*

PSALM 132:16

O Mary, Mother of Jesus Christ and Mother of priests, accept this title which we bestow on you to celebrate your motherhood and to contemplate with you the priesthood of your Son and of your sons, O holy Mother of God.

O Mother of Christ, to the Messiah-priest you gave a body of flesh through the anointing of the Holy Spirit for the salvation of the poor and the contrite of heart; guard priests in your heart and in the Church, O Mother of the Saviour.

O Mother of Faith, you accompanied to the Temple the Son of Man, the fulfilment of the promises given to the fathers; give to the Father for His glory the priests of your Son, O Ark of the Covenant.

O Mother of the Church, in the midst of the disciples in the Upper Room you prayed to the Spirit for the new people and their shepherds; obtain for the Order of Presbyters a full measure of gifts, O Queen of the Apostles.

O Mother of Jesus Christ, you were with Him at the beginning of His life and mission, you sought the Master among the crowd, you stood beside Him when He was lifted up from the earth consumed as the one eternal sacrifice, and you had John, your son, near at hand.

Accept from the beginning those who have been called, protect their growth, in their life ministry accompany your sons, O Mother of priests, Amen.   [PDV n. 82]

FOR PRIESTS AS PASTORS

"And I will give you shepherds after my own heart, who will feed you with knowledge and understanding."

JEREMIAH 3:15

May your every word and deed be an eloquent witness—to our God who is rich in mercy.

May your sermons inspire hope in the mercy of the Redeemer.

May the way you celebrate the sacrament of Penance help each person experience in a unique way the merciful love of God, which is more powerful than sin.

And may your own personal kindness and pastoral love help everyone you meet to discover the merciful Father, who is always ready to forgive.   [OR 3-9-81, 5, 6]

A PRAYER OF PRIESTS TO
CHRIST IN THE EUCHARIST

To this end we always pray for you, that our God may make you worthy of His call, and may fulfil every good resolve and work of faith by His power, so that the name of our Lord Jesus may be glorified in you, and you in Him, according to the grace of our God and the Lord Jesus Christ.

2 THESSALONIANS 1:11-12

Let us pray for our spiritual families, for those entrusted to our ministry. Let us pray particularly for those who in a special way expect our prayers and are in need of them. May our fidelity to prayer ensure that Christ will become ever more the life of our souls.

O great Sacrament of Faith, O holy Priesthood of the Redeemer of the World! Lord Jesus Christ, how grateful we are to You for having brought us into communion with You, for having made us one community around You, for allowing us to celebrate Your unbloody sacrifice and to be ministers of the sacred mysteries in every place: at the altar, in the confessional, the pulpit, the sickroom, the prisons, the classroom, the lecture hall, the offices where we work.

All praise to the Most Holy Eucharist!

[TPS 39/6, 1994, 360]

HOLY THURSDAY PRAYER OF THE PRIESTHOOD

For I received from the Lord what I also delivered to you, that the Lord Jesus on the night when He was betrayed took bread, and when He had given thanks, He broke it, and said, "This is My body which is for you. Do this in remembrance of Me." In the same way also the cup, after supper, saying, "This cup is the new covenant in My blood. Do this, as often as you drink it, in remembrance of Me." For as often as you eat this bread and drink this cup, you proclaim the Lord's death until He comes.

1 CORINTHIANS 11:23-26

We thank You, O Christ;

— because You Yourself have chosen us, associating us in a special way with Your priesthood and marking us with an indelible character which makes each of us able to offer Your own sacrifice as the sacrifice of the whole people: a sacrifice of reconciliation, in which You unceasingly offer to the Father Your own self, and—in You—man and the world;

— because You have made us ministers of the Eucharist and of Your pardon; sharers in Your mission of evangelization; servants of the people of the New Covenant ...

Each one of us is aware that through the Holy Spirit, working through the power of Your cross and resurrection, we have received the ministerial priesthood in order to serve the cause of man's salvation in Your Church; and so:

— we ask today, on this day which is so holy for us, that Your priesthood may be continually renewed in the Church, through Your Spirit, who in every epoch of history must "preserve the youth" of this beloved Bride of Yours;

— we ask that each one of us will find again in his heart, and will unceasingly confirm through his life, the genuine meaning that his personal priestly vocation has both for himself and for all people;

—so that in an ever more mature way he may see with the eyes of faith the true dimension and beauty of the priesthood;

—that he may persevere in giving thanks for the gift of his vocation, as for an undeserved grace;

—so that, giving thanks unceasingly, he may be strengthened in fidelity to this holy gift, which—precisely because it is completely gratuitous—imposes a proportionately greater obligation ...

We beg:

— that our priesthood may be renewed by the power of the Holy Spirit;

— that it may be ever vibrant with a humble but solid certainty of our vocation and mission;

— that our readiness for the sacred sacrifice may increase.

O Christ of the Upper Room and of Calvary! Accept us all ... and by the mystery of Holy Thursday sanctify us anew. Amen. [OR 4-5, 12-82, 1, 3]

FOR THE WORK OF CATECHESIS

We have not ceased to pray for you, asking that you may be filled with the knowledge of His will in all spiritual wisdom and understanding, to lead a life worthy of the Lord, fully pleasing to Him, bearing fruit in every good work and increasing in the knowledge of God.

COLOSSIANS 1:9-10

Catechesis, which is growth in faith and the maturing of Christian life towards its fullness, is ... a work of the Holy Spirit, a work that He alone can initiate and sustain in the Church ... To invoke this Spirit constantly, to be in communion with Him, to endeavour to know His authentic inspirations must be the attitude of the teaching Church and of every catechist ...

I invoke on the catechizing Church this Spirit of the Father and the Son, and I beg Him to renew catechetical dynamism in the Church ...

May the presence of the Holy Spirit, through the

prayers of Mary, grant the Church unprecedented enthusiasm in the catechetical work that is essential for her. Thus
will she effectively carry out, at this moment of grace,
her inalienable and universal mission, the mission given
her by her Teacher: "Go therefore and make disciples of
all nations."[9]

[CT n. 72, 73]

FOR THOSE WHO ARE BAPTIZED

Do you not know that all of us who have been baptized into Christ Jesus were baptized into His death? We were buried therefore with Him by baptism into death, so that as Christ was raised from the dead by the glory of the Father, we too might walk in newness of life.

ROMANS 6:3-4

Let us pray today for all those who will receive Baptism, whether they be newly born—who through this sacrament begin to participate in the faith of the Church through the action of their parents—or whether they be adult catechumens.

Let us pray that the significance of this sacrament may deepen and grow stronger.

Let us ask that it become the gate of faith and of unity of the People of God, of the Church …

May [there] continually and always be developed in us that which was implanted by the grace of Baptism.

The whole Christian life is, in a certain sense, a gradual and constant collaboration with that mysterious beginning of divine life received in baptism.

Let us pray, then, for all the Baptized so that the grace of this sacrament be not received by them in vain,[10] but constantly bear abundant fruits.   [OR 9-13-82, 1]

FOR THE MISSION OF THE LAITY

Now there are varieties of gifts, but the same Spirit; and there are varieties of service, but the same Lord; and there are varieties of working, but it is the same God who inspires them all in everyone. To each is given the manifestation of the Spirit for the common good.

1 CORINTHIANS 12:4-7

O Most Blessed Virgin Mary, Mother of Christ and Mother of the Church, with joy and wonder we seek to make our own your *Magnificat*, joining you in your hymn of thankfulness and love. With you we give thanks to God, "whose mercy is from generation to generation",[11] for the exalted vocation, and the many forms of mission entrusted to the lay faithful. God has called each of them by name to live His own communion of love and holiness and to be one in the great family of God's children. He has sent them forth to shine with the light of Christ and to communicate the fire of the Spirit in every part of society through their life inspired by the Gospel.

54

O Virgin of the *Magnificat*, fill their hearts with a gratitude and enthusiasm for this vocation and mission. With humility and magnanimity you were the "handmaid of the Lord";[12] give us your unreserved willingness for service to God and the salvation of the world. Open our hearts to the great anticipation of the Kingdom of God and of the proclamation of the Gospel to the whole of creation.

Your mother's heart is ever mindful of the many dangers and evils which threaten to overpower men and women in our time. At the same time your heart also takes notice of the many initiatives undertaken for good, the great yearning for values, and the progress achieved in bringing forth the abundant fruits of salvation.

O Virgin full of courage, may your spiritual strength and trust in God inspire us, so that we might know how to overcome all the obstacles that we encounter in accomplishing our mission. Teach us to treat the affairs of the world with a real sense of Christian responsibility and a joyful hope of the coming of God's Kingdom, and of a "new heavens and a new earth".[13] You who were gathered in prayer with the apostles in the Cenacle, awaiting the coming of the Spirit at Pentecost, implore His renewed outpouring on all the faithful, men and women alike, so that they might more fully respond to their vocation and mission, as branches engrafted to the true vine, called to bear much fruit for the life of the world.

O Virgin Mother, guide and sustain us so that we might always live as true sons and daughters of the Church of your Son. Enable us to do our part in helping to establish on earth the civilization of truth and love as God wills it, for His glory. Amen.   [CL 64]

FOR HELP IN TURNING OUTWARD TO OTHERS

So we are ambassadors for Christ, God making His appeal through us.

2 CORINTHIANS 5:20

Spouse of the Holy Spirit and Seat of Wisdom, ... help us in the great endeavour that we are carrying out to meet on a more and more mature way our brothers in the faith, with whom so many things unite us, although there is still something dividing us. Through all the means of knowledge, of mutual respect, of love, of shared collaboration in various fields, may we be able to rediscover gradually the divine plan for the unity into which we should enter and bring everybody in, in order that the one fold of Christ may recognize and live its unity on earth. Mother of unity, teach us constantly the ways that lead to unity.

Allow us in the future to go out to meet human beings and all the peoples that are seeking God and wishing to serve Him on the way of different religions. Help us all to proclaim Christ and reveal "the power of God and the wisdom of God"[14] hidden in His cross. You were the first to reveal Him at Bethlehem, not only to the simple faithful shepherds but also to the wise men from distant lands.

Mother of Good Counsel, show us always how we are to serve the individual and humanity in every nation, how we are to lead them along the ways of salvation. How we are to protect justice and peace in a world continually threatened on various sides. How greatly I desire ... to entrust to you all the difficult problems of the societies, systems, and states—problems that cannot be solved with hatred, war, and self-destruction, but only by peace, justice, and respect for the rights of people and nations.   [OR 6-11-79, 12]

FOR RESPONSES TO GOD'S CALL

Who then will offer willingly, consecrating himself today to the Lord?

1 CHRONICLES 29:5

Let us pray that the most holy mysteries of the risen Christ and of the Spirit, the Paraclete, may enlighten many generous people, ready to serve the Church with greater readiness. Let us pray for the pastors and their collaborators, that they may find the right words in putting before the faithful the message of the priestly and consecrated life. Let us pray that in all parts of the Church the faithful may believe with renewed fervour in the Gospel ideal of the priest completely dedicated to the building up of the Kingdom of God: and let us pray that they support such vocations with generosity.

Let us pray for the young people, to whom the Lord extends His invitation to follow Him more closely, that they may not be drawn away by the things of this world, but may open their hearts to the loving voice that is calling them. Let us pray that they may feel capable of dedicating themselves for their whole lives, "with undivided heart", to Christ, the Church, and souls. Let us pray that they may believe that grace gives them the strength to make this gift, and that they may see the beauty and greatness of the priestly, religious, and missionary life.

Let us pray for families, that they may succeed in creating a Christian environment favourable to the important religious choices of their children. And at the same time with all our hearts let us thank the Lord that in these recent years, in many parts of the world, many young and not so young people are responding in growing numbers to the divine call.

Let us pray that all priests and religious may be an example and an encouragement to those who have been called, by their availability and humble readiness, ... to accept the gifts of the Holy Spirit and to transmit to others the fruits of love and peace, to give them that certainty of faith from which derive the profound understanding of the meaning of human existence and the capacity to introduce moral order into the life of individuals and of the human setting.

[OR 1-14-80]

TO THE MOTHER OF VOCATIONS

And I heard the voice of the Lord saying, "Whom shall I send, and who will go for us?" Then I said, "Here am I! Send me."

ISAIAH 6:8

We entrust to the Virgin Mary the great cause of consecrated life. Following the invitation of her words, "Do whatever He tells you,"[15] we ask the Mother of Vocations:

O Virgin Mary, to you we commend our young people, in particular the youth called to follow your Son more closely. You know the difficulties, the struggles, the obstacles they must face. Assist them to utter their "yes" to the divine call, as you did at the invitation of the angel. Draw them to your heart so that they can understand with you the beauty and the joy that awaits them when the Omnipotent calls them into His intimacy, to make them witnesses of His love and make them able to inspire the Church with their consecration.

O Virgin Mary, help us to rejoice with you in seeing the love brought by your Son received, treasured, and returned. Grant that we may see even in our own days the wonders of the mysterious action of the Holy Spirit.   [TPS 37/3, 1992, 131]

FOR SPIRITUAL LABOURERS

I urge you therefore, brothers, by the mercies of God, to offer your bodies as a living sacrifice, holy and pleasing to God, your spiritual worship. Do not conform yourself to this age but be transformed by the renewal of your mind, that you may discern what is the will of God, what is good and pleasing and perfect.

ROMANS 12:1-2 NAB

May each local Church hear in these words of mine a fresh invitation from Christ to pray the Lord of the harvest "to send labourers into His harvest".[16] And so, dear brothers and sons and daughters, let us join in a prayer as wide as the world, as strong as our faith, as persevering as the love that the Holy Spirit has poured out into our hearts; through this prayer:

— *let us praise the Lord,* who has enriched His Church with the gift of the priesthood, with the many different forms of consecrated life and with numberless other graces, for the building up of His people and for the service of humanity;

— *let us give thanks to the Lord,* who continues to send out His call, to which many young people and others, in these years and in various parts of the world, are responding with growing generosity;

— *let us ask pardon of the Lord* for our weaknesses and infidelities, which perhaps discourage others from responding to His call;

— *let us fervently ask the Lord* to grant to pastors, to religious, to missionaries and other consecrated persons the gifts of wisdom, counsel, and prudence in calling others to the total service of God and the Church. May He also grant to ever more numerous young people and others not so young the generosity and courage to respond and to persevere.

Let us all offer this humble and trusting prayer, entrusting it to the intercession of Mary, Mother of the Church, Queen of the clergy, the shining model for every person consecrated to the service of the People of God.   [OR 4-27-81]

FOR LABOURERS IN THE HARVEST

Then He said to His disciples, "The harvest is plentiful, but the labourers are few; pray therefore the Lord of the harvest to send out labourers into His harvest."

MATTHEW 9:37-38

Let us listen to the words of our Lord Jesus Christ, who says: "Lift up your eyes, and see how the fields are already white for harvest. He who reaps receives wages, and gathers fruit for eternal life, so that sower and reaper may rejoice together."[17]

And let us ask—let us ask Him with our whole soul for this reaping, just as the Samaritan woman asked to have living water, water for eternal life.[18] And looking at "the fields already white for harvest", let us think that harvesters are needed just as sowers were first needed. And let us say to Christ who redeemed us with His blood: Lord, here I am! Take me as sower and as reaper in Your Kingdom. Lord, here I am! Send labourers to the harvest. "Send out labourers into your harvest."[19]

May our consciences be renewed ... and may the zeal of the true disciples of Christ be revived.   [OR 4-6-81, 12]

FOR TEACHERS AND STUDENTS OF THEOLOGY

You, then . . . be strong in the grace that is in Christ Jesus, and what you have heard from me before many witnesses entrust to faithful men who will be able to teach others also.

2 TIMOTHY 2:1-2

To our common Mother, Seat of Wisdom, I commend your persons and your labours. May it be she—who so profoundly knew her Son and so faithfully followed Him—who always guides you on the road to Jesus.

May you live what you study and learn. In the professor's chair and in your publications, may there never be anything which does not accord with the faith of the Church and the directives of the Magisterium. May you feel the joy and the ecclesial responsibility of giving the authentic doctrine of Christ to those who will communicate it to others. May you be true servants of Him who is the light, truth, and salvation.   [OR 12-20-82, 4]

FOR THE EFFECTIVENESS OF THE GOSPEL

Now I am reminding you, brothers, of the gospel I preached to you, which you indeed received and in which you also stand. Through it, you are also being saved, if you hold fast to the word I preached to you . . .

1 CORINTHIANS 15:1-2 NAB

May our sins be taken away through the words of the Gospel.

May the words of the Gospel help us to taste the things of God and read the depths of mysteries.

May the word of the Gospel let us rediscover the hope of our calling. [OR 10-18-82, 2]

FOR THE FAITH OF GOD'S PEOPLE

Be watchful, stand firm in your faith, be courageous, be strong.

1 CORINTHIANS 16:13

May your faith be strong; may it not hesitate, not waver, before the doubts, the uncertainties which philosophical systems or fashionable movements would like to suggest to you. May it not descend to compromise with certain concepts, which would like to present Christianity as a mere ideology of historical character, and therefore to be placed at the same level as so many others, now outdated.

May your faith be joyful, because it is based on awareness of possessing a divine gift. When you pray and dialogue with God and when you converse with men, [may you] manifest the joy of this enviable possession.   [OR 11-3-80, 3]

FOR THE PARISH

*For just as the body is one and has many
members, and all the members of the body,
though many, are one body, so it is with Christ.
For by one Spirit we were all baptized into one
body . . . and all were made to drink of one Spirit
. . . Now you are the body of Christ and individ-
ually members of it.*

1 CORINTHIANS 12:12-13, 27

May spouses pray for the grace of perseverance in conju-
gal faithfulness and in that of parents. May they pray to
obtain the love necessary to carry out the vocation they
have received from God.

May children find in this parish a vaster family home.
May they absorb in catechesis the truth of the word of
God. May they be nourished with the Body of the Saviour.

May the young seek in this parish support for their
ideals and commit themselves to animating with their

new life, with their witness, with readiness to serve God and man.

May the sick and the suffering find consolation and relief here. May Christ visit them, by means of the service of the priests, and explain to them with the interior word of the Spirit the great dignity and significance of their sufferings.

May all in this parish become aware of being members of the Body of Christ and realize that the Kingdom of God is approaching them—that, in fact, it is already present in them.

I pray for all these today, together with you, trusting above all in the intercession of Mary, who is Mother of the Church and the cause of our joy.   [OR 12-17-79]

LEAD US IN TRUTH

On the way of wisdom I direct you,
I lead you on straightforward paths.
When you walk, your step will not be impeded,
and should you run, you will not stumble.

PROVERBS 4:11-12 NAB

Lead us in truth!

Lead in truth, O Christ, the fathers and mothers of families in the parish. Urged on and strengthened by the sacramental grace of marriage, and aware of being on earth the visible sign of your unfailing love for the Church, let them be serene and firm in shouldering with evangelical consistency the responsibilities of married life and of the Christian upbringing of their children.

Lead in truth, O Christ, the young people of the parish. Let them not be attracted by the new idols, such as exaggerated consumerism, prosperity at all costs, moral permissiveness, protest expressed with violence, but [rather let them] live with joy your message, which is the message of the Beatitudes, the message of love for God and one's neighbour, the message of moral commitment for the real transformation of society.

Lead in truth, O Christ, all the faithful of the parish. May Christian faith animate their whole life and make them become, before the world, courageous witnesses to Your mission of salvation, responsible and dynamic members of the Church, happy to be sons of God and brothers—with You—of all men!

Lead us in truth, O Christ, always! [OR 12-24-79, 12]

FOR FAITHFULNESS TO THE CROSS

But far be it from me to glory except in the cross of our Lord Jesus Christ, by which the world has been crucified to me, and I to the world.

GALATIANS 6:14

Dear brothers and sisters, may the cross of Christ never forsake you as the source of certainty that "God so loved the world" on it, that He loved man.

May the hope of eternal life never forsake you.

Do not cease reaching out toward it, loving the light—and always drawing near to it. To this light which is the cross of Christ. And His resurrection. To the light that is Christ Himself.[20] Amen. [OR 3-29-82, 11]

FOR MORAL RENEWAL

*A clean heart create for me, O God,
and a steadfast spirit renew within me . . .
Steady my footsteps according to Your promise,
and let no iniquity rule over me.*

PSALM 51:12; 119:133 NAB

O Mary, Mother of Mercy, watch over all people, that the cross of Christ may not be emptied of its power, that man may not stray from the path of the good or become blind to sin, but may put his hope ever more fully in God who is "rich in mercy".[21]

May he carry out the good works prepared by God beforehand[22] and so live completely "for the praise of His glory".[23]   [VS n. 120]

FOR A RENEWAL OF PENANCE

He who conceals his transgressions
*   will not prosper,*
but he who confesses and forsakes them
will obtain mercy.

PROVERBS 28:13

I entrust to the Father, rich in mercy, I entrust to the
Son of God, made man as our Redeemer and reconciler, I
entrust to the Holy Spirit, source of unity and peace, this
call of mine, as father and pastor, to penance and reconciliation. May the most holy and adorable Trinity cause to
spring up in the Church and in the world the small seed
which at this hour I plant in the generous soil of so many
human hearts.

In order that in the not-too-distant future abundant
fruits may come from it, I invite you all to join me in
turning to Christ's heart, the eloquent sign of the divine
mercy, the "propitiation for our sins", "our peace and
reconciliation",[24] that we may draw from it an interior

encouragement to hate sin and to be converted to God, and find in it the divine kindness which lovingly responds to human repentance.

I likewise invite you to turn with me to the immaculate heart of Mary, Mother of Jesus, in whom "is effected the reconciliation of God with humanity, ... is accomplished the work of reconciliation, because she has received from God the fullness of grace in virtue of the redemptive sacrifice of Christ."[25] Truly Mary has been associated with God, by virtue of her divine motherhood, in the work of reconciliation.[26]

Into the hands of this mother, whose fiat marked the beginning of the "fullness of time"[27] in which Christ accomplished the reconciliation of humanity with God, to her immaculate heart—to which we have repeatedly entrusted the whole of humanity, disturbed by sin and tormented by so many tensions and conflicts—I now in a special way entrust this intention: that through her intercession humanity may discover and travel the path of penance, the only path that can lead it to full reconciliation.

[RP n. 35]

FOR CONFESSION OF SIN

Have mercy on me, O God, in Your goodness; in the greatness of Your compassion wipe out my offence.
Thoroughly wash me from my guilt and of my sin cleanse me.
For I acknowledge my offence, and my sin is before me always:
"Against You only have I sinned, and done what is evil in Your sight" …
Behold, You are pleased with sincerity of heart, and in my inmost being You teach me wisdom.

PSALM 51:3-6, 8 NAB

O Immaculate Virgin, Mother of the true God and Mother of the Church! … Hear the prayer that we address to you with filial trust, and present it to your Son Jesus, our sole Redeemer …

Our hope, look upon us with compassion, teach us to go continually to Jesus and, if we fall, help us to rise again, to return to Him, by means of the confession of our faults and sins in the sacrament of Penance, which gives peace to the soul. We beg you to grant us a great love for all the holy sacraments, which are, as it were, the signs that your Son left us on earth.

Thus, most holy Mother, with the peace of God in our conscience, with our hearts free from evil and hatred, we will be able to bring all true joy and true peace, which come to us from your Son, our Lord Jesus Christ, who with God the Father and the Holy Spirit, lives and reigns for ever and ever. Amen.   [OR 1-29-79]

TO ABIDE IN GOD'S LOVE

"As the Father has loved Me, so have I loved you; abide in My love. If you keep My commandments, you will abide in My love."

JOHN 15:9-10

Yes, beloved brothers and sisters, let us not tire of casting the seed of our work, however humble it may be, looking up towards the sky which, even when it is covered with clouds, contains the sun which will reappear, even after storms.

The Church looks to us. Christ looks to us, and awaits daily commitment from us. And the Father prays for us: *Ut unum sint.* ["That they may be one."]

"The glory which thou hast given me I have given to them, that they may be one even as We are one, I in them and Thou in me, that they may become perfectly one, so that the world may know that Thou hast sent Me and hast loved them even as Thou hast loved Me."[28]

Let us abide in this love. Let us live in this love. Let us operate in this love.

In the love of the Father, the Son, and the Holy Spirit. May it give us every day the sense of the universal dimension of our service.

For the whole Church.

For all brothers with whom we are not yet one.

For the whole world.

Ut unum sint ... ut credat mundus. ["That they may be one ... that the world may believe."]   [OR 2-2-81, 2]

V

PRAYERS FOR THE FAMILY

*Unless the Lord builds the house,
those who build it labour in vain.*

PSALM 127:1

FOR EVERY FAMILY ON EARTH

*Blessed is everyone who fears the Lord,
who walks in His ways!...
Your wife will be like a fruitful vine within your
house;
your children will be like olive shoots around
your table.
Lo, thus shall the man be blessed who fears the
Lord.*

PSALM 128:1, 3-4

Lord, from You every family in heaven and on earth takes its name.[1] Father, You are Love and Life.

Through Your Son, Jesus Christ, born of woman, and through the Holy Spirit, the fountain of divine charity, grant that every family on earth may become for each successive generation a true shrine of life and love.

Grant that Your grace may guide the thoughts and actions of husbands and wives for the good of their families and of all the families in the world.

Grant that the young may find in the family solid support for their human dignity and for their growth in truth and love.

Grant that love, strengthened by the grace of the sacrament of Marriage, may prove mightier than all the weaknesses and trials through which our families sometimes pass.

Through the intercession of the Holy Family of Nazareth, grant that the Church may fruitfully carry out her worldwide mission in the family and through the family.

We ask this of You, who are Life, Truth, and Love with the Son and the Holy Spirit. Amen.   [OR 5-25-80, 19]

FOR "THE CHURCH OF THE HOME"

Choose this day whom you will serve ... As for me and my house, we will serve the Lord.

JOSHUA 24:15

Saint Joseph was "a just man", a tireless worker, the upright guardian of those entrusted to his care. May he always guard, protect, and enlighten families.

May the Virgin Mary, who is Mother of the Church, also be the Mother of "the church of the home". Thanks to her motherly aid, may each Christian family really become a "little church" in which the mystery of the Church is mirrored and given new life. May she, the handmaid of the Lord, be an example of humble and generous acceptance of the will of God. May she, the sorrowful Mother at the foot of the cross, comfort the sufferings and dry the tears of those in distress because of the difficulties of their families.

May Christ the Lord, the universal King, the King of families, be present in every home as He was at Cana, bestowing light, joy, serenity, and strength ... I beg of Him that every family may generously make its own contribution to the coming of His Kingdom in the world—"a Kingdom of truth and life, a Kingdom of holiness and grace, a Kingdom of justice, love and peace",[2] toward which history is journeying.

I entrust each family to Him, to Mary and to Joseph.

[FC n. 86]

FOR PRAYER IN THE FAMILY

For where two or three are gathered in my name, there am I in the midst of them.

MATTHEW 18:20

May the prayer of the Church, the prayer of families as domestic churches, constantly rise up! May it make itself heard first by God and then also by people everywhere, so that they will not succumb to doubt, and all who are wavering because of human weakness will not yield to the tempting glamour of merely apparent goods, like those held out in every temptation.

Let us pray for families throughout the world. Let us pray, through Christ, with Him and in Him, to the Father "from whom every family in heaven and on earth is named".[3]

[TPS 39/4, 1994, 211]

FOR THE HELP OF THE HOLY FAMILY

And when they had performed everything according to the law of the Lord, they returned to Galilee, to their own city, Nazareth. And the Child [Jesus] grew and became strong, filled with wisdom; and the favour of God was upon Him.

LUKE 2:39-40

May the Holy Family, icon and model of every human family, help each individual to walk in the spirit of Nazareth. May it help each family unit to grow in understanding of its particular mission in society and the Church by hearing the word of God, by prayer, and by a fraternal sharing of life. May Mary, Mother of Fairest Love, and Joseph, guardian of the Redeemer, accompany us all with their constant protection.

With these sentiments I bless every family in the name of the Most Holy Trinity: Father, Son, and Holy Spirit.

[TPS 39/4, 1994, 243-4]

VI

PRAYERS FOR GROUPS WITH SPECIAL CONCERNS

Answer me when I call, O God . . .
Be gracious to me, and hear my prayer.

PSALM 4:1

THANKSGIVING FOR WOMEN

A woman who fears the Lord is to be praised.
Give her the fruit of her hands,
and let her works praise her in the gates.

PROVERBS 31:30-31

The Church desires to give thanks to the Most Holy Trinity for the mystery of woman and for every woman— for that which constitutes the eternal measure of her feminine dignity, for the great works of God which throughout human history have been accomplished in her and through her. After all, was it not in and through her that the greatest event in human history—the incarnation of God Himself—was accomplished?

Therefore the Church gives thanks for each and every woman: for mothers, for sisters, for wives; for women consecrated to God in virginity; for women dedicated to the many human beings who await the gratuitous love of another person; for women who watch over the human persons in the family ... for women who work professionally, and who at times are burdened by a great social responsibility; for "perfect" women and for "weak" women—for all women as they have come forth from the heart of God in all the beauty and richness of their femininity; as they have been embraced by His eternal love; as, together with men, they are pilgrims on this earth ... as they assume, together with men, a common responsibility for the destiny of humanity according to daily necessities and according to that definitive destiny which the human family has in God Himself, in the bosom of the ineffable Trinity.

The Church gives thanks for all the manifestations of the feminine genius which have appeared in the course of history, in the midst of all peoples and nations; she gives thanks for all the charisms which the Holy Spirit distributes to women in the history of the People of God, for all the victories which she owes to their faith, hope, and charity: she gives thanks for all the fruits of feminine holiness.

The Church asks at the same time that these invaluable "manifestations of the Spirit",[1] which with great generosity are poured forth upon the daughters of the eternal Jerusalem, may be attentively recognized and appreciated so that they may return for the common good of the Church and of humanity, especially in our times. Meditating on the biblical mystery of the woman, the Church prays that in this mystery all women may discover themselves and their supreme vocation.   [MD n. 31]

FOR CHILDREN

Jesus said, "Let the children come to Me, and do not hinder them; for to such belongs the kingdom of heaven."

MATTHEW 19:14

May the Blessed Virgin, who had the joy of bringing and holding in her arms the Son of God made a Child, of seeing Him grow in wisdom, age, and grace before God and man,[2] help each one [of us] to endow his personal efforts on behalf of little children with active goodness, an attractive example, and self-giving love.   [TPS 39/3, 1994, 169]

FOR YOUNG PEOPLE

*he Lord said to me, "Do not say, 'I am only
a youth'; for to all to whom I send you you
shall go, and whatever I command you you shall
speak. Be not afraid of them, for I am with you to
deliver you, says the Lord." Then the Lord put
forth His hand and touched my mouth ...*

JEREMIAH 1:7-8

"Go," [Jesus said,] " ... and proclaim the Good News."³
Let us earnestly pray to the Lord of the harvest that the
youth of the world will not hesitate to reply: "Here am I!
Send me! Send us!" Amen. [TPS 39/1, 1994, 5]

Lord Jesus Christ!

Put new life into the hearts of young people ... Saint
John writes that the love You give is the "light of men"⁴ ...
Let their light shine for all peoples: for their families, for
their cultures and societies, for their economic and political
systems, for the whole international order.

Coming into the room where the disciples were gathered, after Your resurrection, You said: "Peace be with you!"[5] Make ... young people bearers of your peace. Teach them the meaning of what You said on the mountain: "Blest are the peacemakers, for they shall be called sons and daughters of God."[6]

Send them as the Father sent You: to free their brothers and sisters from fear and sin; for the glory of our Heavenly Father. Amen.   [TPS 40/3, 1995]

FOR THOSE WHO ARE ILL

Why are you cast down, O my soul,
and why are you disquieted within me?
Hope in God, for I shall again praise Him,
my help and my God.

PSALM 42:5

Lord, with the faith You have given us, we acknowledge that You are God Almighty, our Creator and provident Father, the God of hope, in Jesus Christ our Saviour, the God of love in the Holy Spirit our Comforter!

Lord, trusting in Your promises, which do not pass away, we want to come always to You, and to find in You relief in our suffering. However, disciples of Jesus as we are, let not our will but Yours be done throughout our whole life!

Lord, grateful for Christ's preference for the lepers who had the good fortune to come into contact with Him, seeing ourselves in them ... we also thank You for the favours we receive in everything that helps us, gives us relief, and consoles us. We thank You for the medicine and the doctors, for the care of the nurses, for the circumstances of life, for those who console us and are consoled by us, for those who understand and accept us, and for the others.

Lord, grant us patience, serenity, and courage; grant that we may live a joyful charity, for love of You, towards those who are suffering more than we and towards those who, though not suffering, have not grasped the meaning of life.

Lord, we ask that our life be useful, we want to serve: to praise, to give thanks, to atone, and to implore with Christ, for those who worship You and for those who do not worship You in the world, and for the Church, scattered all over the earth.

Lord, through the infinite merits of Christ on the cross, a "Suffering Servant" and our brother with whom we unite, we pray to You for our families, our friends, and benefactors … Amen.   [OR 8-11-80, 3]

FOR THE SPECIAL MISSION FOR THE SICK

Now I rejoice in my sufferings for your sake,
and in my flesh I complete what is lacking
in Christ's afflictions for the sake of His body, that
is, the Church.

COLOSSIANS 1:24

I address a particularly affectionate and respectful thought to the sick. How could I not feel sincere and fatherly affection for those who, in any family or institute, perhaps in solitude, are sorely tried by painful physical and spiritual afflictions? But my greeting to you, dear sick people, besides being affectionate, is also respectful, because you are among us a special presence of the Lord. You possess a particular likeness to Christ the Redeemer; you have an extraordinary mission of salvation and sanctification, for yourselves and others.

May the Lord comfort you with the riches of His grace.

May He free you, if it is His will, from your tribulations.

May He give you serenity and courage, and so much faith and so much hope. [OR 11-26-79, 12]

FOR THE DISABLED

If we are afflicted, it is for your encouragement and salvation.

2 CORINTHIANS 1:6 NAB

In Jesus Christ there is an important message for all the disabled, and for those who serve the disabled, and for society as a whole in its relations with them. Jesus Christ brought us a message that has emphasized the absolute value of life and of the human person, who comes from God and is called to live in communion with God. The same message can be read in His own life of love for the sick and suffering, and of service to them.

The message also comes from the words with which He identified Himself with all those in need and indicated that His disciples should be known for their loving service of the poor and the weak: "As you did it to one of the least of these my brethren, you did it to me."[7]

I pray that His message will be heard, and that fresh hope will be given to the disabled, and that new love will permeate all society.   [OR 4-21-81, 8]

FOR ALL THE SUFFERING

He said to me, "My grace is sufficient for you, for My power is made perfect in weakness." I will all the more gladly boast of my weaknesses, that the power of Christ may rest upon me.

2 CORINTHIANS 12:9-10

The sick, the elderly, the handicapped, and the dying teach us that weakness is a creative part of human living, and that suffering can be embraced with no loss of dignity. Without the presence of these people in your midst you might be tempted to think of health, strength, and power as the only important values to be pursued in life. *But the wisdom of Christ and the power of Christ are to be seen in the weakness of those who share His sufferings.*

Let us keep the sick and the handicapped at the centre of our lives. Let us treasure them and recognize with gratitude the debt we owe them. We begin by imagining that we are giving to them; we end by realizing that they have enriched us.

May God bless and comfort all who suffer. And may Jesus Christ, the Saviour of the world and healer of the sick, make His light shine through human weakness as a beacon for us and for all mankind. Amen. [OR 5-31-82, 3]

FOR THE HUNGRY

Is this not the fast that I choose:
to loose the bonds of wickedness,
to undo the thongs of the yoke,
to let the oppressed go free,
and to break every yoke?
Is it not to share your bread with the hungry,
and bring the homeless poor into your house;
when you see the naked, to cover him,
and not to hide yourself from your own flesh?

ISAIAH 58:6-8

In the richer countries many selfishly consume more than is shared by others of the fruits of nature which God has granted to all mankind. We must therefore note with sorrow that there are still millions of people in the whole world who suffer chronically from hunger ...

We pray that the cry of the poor and the starving may

be heard and that in a spirit of true brotherhood and co-operation the problem of world hunger may finally be overcome.

[OR 10-25-82, 2]

FOR WORKERS

May the gracious care of the Lord our God be ours; prosper the work of our hands for us! Prosper the work of our hands!

PSALM 90:17 NAB

I pray to God ardently for the happiness of all:

— that your just aspirations may be realized;
— that the moments and the reasons of crisis may be overcome;
— that work will never be an alienation for anyone;
— that, on the contrary, it may be honoured by every-one as it deserves, so that justice and even more love may triumph in it;
— that the environment of work will really be fit for man, and that man may be able to appreciate it as an exten-sion of his own family;
— that work may help man to be more of a man;
— and that, with the commitment of everyone, it may be possible to arrive at the construction of a new society and a new world, in the full realization of justice, free-dom, and peace. [OR 3-30-81]

FOR THOSE WHO LABOUR ON FARMS

And if you obey the voice of the Lord your God ... blessed shall be the fruit of your body, and the fruit of your ground, and the fruit of your beasts, the increase of your cattle, and the young of your flock ... The Lord will open to you His good treasury the heavens, to give the rain of your land in its season and to bless all the work of your hands.

DEUTERONOMY 28:1, 4, 12

I wish ... that in this invitation to prayer all men who till the land may find the confirmation of that esteem which the Church has for their work, and which she draws from Christ. It cannot be otherwise, if we remember that Christ once described God, His Father, as "the vinedresser".[8] And therefore, expressing our respect for all farm workers in every part of the world, let us pray to God "the vine-dresser", our heavenly Father, to bless their work, protect

[them] from natural calamities which can destroy its fruit, so that they may be happy to serve their neighbour, supplying him with the necessary foodstuffs.

And let us also pray that He may bless the efforts of all those engaged, at the national and international level, in the advancement and prosperity of the rural world.

[OR 7-23-79, 2]

FOR WORKERS IN THE MASS MEDIA

There is one whose rash words are like sword thrusts,
but the tongue of the wise brings healing . . .
Death and life are in the power of the tongue,
and those who love it will eat its fruits.

PROVERBS 12:18; 18:21

I earnestly invite all media workers to join us in the Church's day of reflection and prayer, [World Communications Day]. We beg the Almighty together to deepen their consciousness of the tremendous opportunity which is theirs to serve mankind and to shape the world towards good. We ask Him to endow them with the understanding, wisdom, and courage which they will always need in bearing their awesome responsibility. We beg Him to keep them always intensely mindful of their audiences, which for the most part are families like their own, with overworked parents often too tired to be alert, and with children who are trusting, impressionable, vulnerable, and easily led.

For, remembering this, they will keep in mind also the enormous consequences which their work may have for good or ill and will not easily be false to themselves or to the principles of their noble calling.   [OR 5-19-80]

FOR EDUCATIONAL AND CULTURAL LEADERS

You are the salt of the earth; but if salt has lost its taste, how shall its saltness be restored? It is no longer good for anything except to be thrown out and trodden under foot by men.

You are the light of the world. A city set on a hill cannot be hidden. Nor do men light a lamp and put it under a bushel, but on a stand, and it gives light to all in the house. Let your light so shine before men, that they may see your good works and give glory to your Father who is in heaven.

MATTHEW 5:13-16

University people, intellectuals, scientists, and men and women of culture: as the Gospel … says, you are the salt of the earth.[9] You must not lose your saviour. You are cities set on hills. You are lights put on lampstands.

Elevate. Educate. Enlighten. Encourage. Animate. The Church understands you and respects you. The Church offers you the right hand of friendship and collaboration.

We are now gathered around the altar of the Master, whose words so often astounded His listeners for their wisdom. Let us all pray to Him for the gift of wisdom. In this eucharistic celebration Christ welcomes and accepts your service of man through culture; He accepts the fruits of your intellectual and artistic activities; He offers·them to the Father as a pleasing sacrifice.

And may Jesus Christ the incarnate Wisdom of God be for each of you the light of your lives. May His truth shine in your minds and find expression on your lips. May His truth fill you with joy and lead you to eternal life. Amen.

[OR 2-22-82, 9]

FOR THOSE WHO HAVE MATERIAL ABUNDANCE

As for the rich in this world, charge them not to be haughty, nor to set their hopes on uncertain riches but on God who richly furnishes us with everything to enjoy. They are to do good, to be rich in good deeds, liberal and generous, thus laying up for themselves a good foundation for the future, so that they may take hold of the life which is life indeed.

1 TIMOTHY 6:17-19

Let those who have a superabundance avoid shutting themselves up in themselves, avoid attachment to their own wealth, avoid spiritual blindness. Let them avoid all this with all their strength.

May the whole truth of the Gospel accompany them constantly and, above all, the truth contained in these words: "Blessed are the poor in spirit, for theirs is the kingdom of heaven."[10]

May this truth make them uneasy.

May it be a continual warning and a challenge for them.

May it not allow them even for a minute to become blind out of selfishness and the satisfaction of their own desires.

[OR 7-14-80, 5]

FOR BOTH RICH AND POOR

The rich and the poor meet together;
the Lord is the maker of them all.

PROVERBS 22:2

"Do not lay up for yourselves treasures on earth, where moth and rust consume and where thieves break in and steal, but lay up for yourselves treasures in heaven."[11] May rich and poor recognize that they are brothers and sisters. May they share what they have with one another as children of the one God who loves everyone, who wills the good of everyone, and who offers to everyone the gift of peace!

[TPS 38/3, 1993, 160-1]

FOR THE JEWISH PEOPLE

The Lord bless you from Zion!
  May you see the prosperity of Jerusalem
all the days of your life!
May you see your children's children!
Peace be upon Israel!

PSALM 128:5-6

Jews and Christians, as children of Abraham, are called to be a blessing for the world[12] by committing themselves together for peace and justice among all men and peoples, with the fullness and depth that God Himself intended us to have, and with the readiness for sacrifices that this high goal may demand ... In the light of this promise and call of Abraham's, I look with you, [the Jews], to the destiny and role of your people among the peoples. I willingly pray with you for the fullness of Shalom [peace] for all your brothers in nationality and in faith, and also for the land to which Jews look with special veneration.

Our century saw the first pilgrimage of a Pope to the Holy Land ... I wish to repeat Paul VI's words on entering

111

Jerusalem: "Implore with us, in your desire and in your prayer, respect and peace upon this unique land, visited by God! Let us pray here together for the grace of a real and deep brotherhood between all men, between all peoples!... May they who love you be blessed. Yes, may peace dwell in your walls, prosperity in your palaces. I pray for peace for you, I desire happiness for you."[13]

May all peoples in Jerusalem soon be reconciled and blessed in Abraham! May He, the ineffable, of whom His creation speaks to us; He, who does not force mankind to goodness, but guides it; He, who manifests Himself in our fate and is silent; He, who chooses all of us as His people; may He guide us along His ways to His future!

Praised be His Name! Amen.   [OR 12-9-80, 6]

VII

PRAYERS FOR PEACE

*May the Lord give strength to His people!
May the Lord bless His people with
peace!*

PSALM 29:11

DELIVER US!

*He shall judge between the nations,
and shall decide for many peoples;
and they shall beat their swords into
    ploughshares,
and their spears into pruning hooks;
nation shall not lift up sword against nation,
neither shall they learn war any more.*

ISAIAH 2:4

"Deliver us from evil!"[1] Reciting these words of Christ's prayer, it is very difficult to give them a different content from the one that opposes peace, that destroys it, that threatens it. Let us pray therefore: Deliver us from war, from hatred, from the destruction of human lives! Do not allow us to kill! Do not allow the use of those means which are in the service of death and destruction, and whose power, range of action, and precision go beyond the limits known hitherto.

114

Do not allow them to be used ever! "Deliver us from evil!" Defend us from war! From any war, Father, who are in heaven. Father of life and Giver of peace, the Pope—the son of a nation which, during its history and especially in our century, has been among those most sorely tried in the horror, the cruelty, and the cataclysm of war—supplicates You. He supplicates You for all the peoples ·in the world, for all countries and for all continents. He supplicates You in the name of Christ, the Prince of Peace.

Mother, you know what it means to clasp in your arms the dead body of your Son, of Him to whom you gave birth. Spare all mothers on this earth the death of their sons, the torments, the slavery, the destruction of war, the persecutions, the concentration camps, the prisons! Keep for them the joy of birth, of sustenance, of the development of man and of his life. In the name of this life, in the name of the birth of the Lord, implore peace for us and justice in the world!

Mother of peace, in all the beauty and majesty of your motherhood, which the Church exalts and the world admires, we pray to you: Be with us at every moment! Let this ... year be a year of peace, in virtue of the birth and death of your Son! Amen.   [OR 1-8-79, 1, 11]

FOR EVERLASTING PEACE

I will appoint peace your governor,
and justice your ruler.
No longer shall violence be heard of in your land,
or plunder and ruin within your boundaries.

ISAIAH 60:17-18 NAB

To the ⬛⬛ator of nature and man, of truth and beauty, I pray:

Hear my voice, for it is the voice of the victims of all wars and violence among individuals and nations.

Hear my voice, for it is the voice of all children who suffer and will suffer when people put their faith in weapons and war.

Hear my voice when I beg You to instil into the hearts of all human beings the wisdom of peace, the strength of justice, and the joy of fellowship.

Hear my voice, for I speak for the multitudes in every country and in every period of history who do not want war and are ready to walk the road of peace.

Hear my voice and grant insight and strength so that we may always respond to hatred with love, to injustice with total dedication to justice, to need with the sharing of self, to war with peace.

O God, hear my voice and grant unto the world Your everlasting peace.   [OR 3-9-81, 14]

FOR PEACEMAKERS

Watch the wholehearted and mark the upright; for there is a future for the man of peace.

PSALM 37:37 NAB

The truth about man pervades the ways of peace and is the condition for all progress in the modern world.

May Almighty God sustain your hearts in peace and infuse peace into your homes. May He give you deep insight and unflinching courage to pursue the goals of truth, the power of peace.

And may the peace that radiates from the children's smiles convince the world of the truth that makes us free.

[OR 2-18-80, 12]

FOR THE PURSUIT OF PEACE

Let us then pursue what leads to peace and to building up one another.

ROMANS 14:19 NAB

I pray that your vision of human dignity will never fail you in the pursuit of peace.

May you always acknowledge the incomparable worth of every human life, even from the very moment of conception.

May you contribute to the building of peace by always appealing to what is most noble in the heart of every person.

And may that peace which reflects the very goodness of God Himself fill your hearts and your homes, thereby encouraging you to be tireless workers in the cause of peace.

[OR 2-16-81, 11]

TO BE AT PEACE AND TO MAKE PEACE

Blessed are the peacemakers, for they will be called children of God.

MATTHEW 5:9 NAB

As I celebrate among you and with you the Eucharist of our Lord Jesus Christ, I wish us to find in it peace with our fellow man. Peace: the fruit of justice. Peace: the fruit of love. How easily this peace is broken!

How often people are divided among themselves, even though they are physically close, even in the same family!

May Christ give us the ability to remain at peace with others. May there be realized in us the words of His Sermon on the Mount: "Blessed are the peacemakers."[2]

May we learn to make peace: and to build up in peace the society of our families, our neighbourhoods, our work-benches, schools, offices, and factories!

Christ, the peacemaker, gives the peoples of this earth the blessing of peace. May they co-operate with it, through justice and love in all the circumstances of life.   [OR 3-9-81, 10]

FOR HOPE THAT PEACE IS POSSIBLE

May the God of hope fill you with all joy and peace in believing, so that by the power of the Holy Spirit you may abound in hope.

ROMANS 15:13

Jesus, I trust in You! ... *Spes contra spem!* [Hope against hope!] With God nothing is impossible!

What is especially possible is conversion, which can change hatred into love and war into peace.

And so our prayer becomes all the more insistent and trusting: Jesus, I trust in You!   [TPS 39/3, 1994, 183]

VIII

PRAYERS FOR THE NATION

If My people who are called by My name humble themselves, and pray and seek My face, and turn from their wicked ways, then I will hear from heaven, and will forgive their sin and heal their land.

2 CHRONICLES 7:14

FOR POLITICAL LEADERS

First of all, then, I urge that supplications, prayers, intercessions, and thanksgivings be made for all men, for kings and all who are in high positions, that we may lead a quiet and peaceable life, godly and respectful in every way.

1 TIMOTHY 2:1-2

I pray that God will grant you discernment and courage, and enable you to join the very many people of goodwill, both in your own country and throughout the world, in blazing new paths, where all can walk hand in hand and together build a renewed world which will truly be a family, the family of peoples. [TPS 39/5, 1994, 297]

FOR PARLIAMENT AND ALL WHO
WORK FOR JUSTICE

Give the king Thy justice, O God,
and Thy righteousness to the royal son!
May he judge Thy people with righteousness,
and Thy poor with justice! ...
May he defend the cause of the poor of the people,
give deliverance to the needy,
and crush the oppressor!

PSALM 72:1, 2, 4

For all of you I pray to Almighty God that He may grant you the gift of wisdom in your decisions, prudence in your words and actions, and compassion in the exercise of the authority that is yours, so that in your noble office you will always render true service to the people.

[OR 12-29-79, 12]

FOR LIFE, LIBERTY, AND JUSTICE

For lack of guidance, a people falls.

PROVERBS 11:14 NAB

If you want equal justice for all, and true freedom and lasting peace, then ... defend life! ... May God guide this nation, and keep alive in it—for endless generations to come—the flame of liberty and justice for all.

May God bless you all!   [TPS 39/2, 1994, 86-87]

FOR CATHOLICS

For "every one who calls upon the name of the Lord will be saved". But how can they call on Him in whom they have not believed? And how can they believe in Him of whom they have not heard? And how can they hear without someone to preach? And how can people preach unless they are sent? As it is written, "How beautiful are the feet of those who bring [the] good news!"

ROMANS 10:13-15 NAB

I pray with you that you will continue to use responsibly your precious freedom, not only to deepen the faith in those already within the fold, but also to share the faith with the multitude of the unchurched in your country who are ripe for the harvest. For, consciously or not, every man and woman is waiting to be gathered into one fold under one Shepherd. After all, your freedom would be a selfish boast if you did not use it to respond to the unspoken plea of your brothers and sisters in your midst, who are yearning to hear the good news, the message from Jesus Christ.

[OR 6-22-81, 11]

AT THE SHRINE OF THE IMMACULATE CONCEPTION

*ighteousness exalts a nation,
but sin is a reproach to any people.*

PROVERBS 14:34

Today, as I thank you, Mother, for this presence of yours in the midst of the men and women of this land... giving a new form to their social and civic lives, I commend them all to your Immaculate Heart ...

I commend to you, Mother of Christ, and I entrust to you the Catholic Church: the bishops, priests, deacons, individual religious and religious institutes, the seminarians, vocations, and the apostolate of the laity in its various aspects.

In a special way I entrust to you the well-being of the Christian families of this country, the innocence of children, the future of the young, the vocation of single men and women. I ask you to communicate to all ... women ... a deep sharing in the joy that you experienced in your closeness to Jesus Christ, your Son. I ask you to preserve all of them in freedom from sin and evil, like the freedom which was yours in a unique way from the moment of supreme liberation in your Immaculate Conception.

I entrust to you the great work of ecumenism here, in this land, in which those who confess Christ belong to different Churches and communions. I do this in order that the words of Christ's prayer may be fulfilled: "That they may be one." I entrust to you the consciences of men and women and the voice of public opinion, in order that they may not be opposed to the law of God but follow it as the fount of truth and good.

I add to this, Mother, the great cause of justice and peace in the modern world, in order that the force and energy of love may prevail over hatred and destructiveness, and in order that the children of light may not lack concern for the welfare of the whole human family.

Mother, I commend and entrust to you all that goes to make up earthly progress, asking that it should not be one-sided, but that it should create conditions for the full advancement of individuals, families, communities, and nations. I commend to you the poor, the suffering, the sick and the handicapped, the ageing and the dying. I ask you to reconcile those in sin, to heal those in pain, and to uplift those who have lost their hope and joy. Show to those who struggle in doubt the light of Christ your Son.

At a time when the struggle between good and evil, between the prince of darkness and father of lies, and evangelical love is growing more acute, may the light of your Immaculate Conception show to all the way to grace and to salvation. Amen.   [OR 11-5-79, 4]

IX

PRAYERS FOR THE DEFENCE OF LIFE

I have set before you life and death, blessing and curse; therefore choose life, that you and your descendants may live.

DEUTERONOMY 30:19

FOR REVERENCE FOR LIFE

*$\mathcal{H}$ow precious is Your love, O God!...
For with You is the fountain of life,
and in Your light we see light.*

PSALM 36:8, 10 NAB

Jesus proclaims that life finds its centre, its meaning and its fulfilment when it is given up ... We too are called to give our lives for our brothers and sisters, and thus to realize in the fullness of truth the meaning and destiny of our existence.

We shall be able to do this because You, O Lord, have given us the example and have bestowed on us the power of Your Spirit. We shall be able to do this if every day, with You and like You, we are obedient to the Father and do His will.

Grant, therefore, that we may listen with open and generous hearts to every word which proceeds from the mouth of God. Thus shall we learn not only to obey the commandment not to kill human life, but also to revere life, to love it, and to foster it. [EV n. 51]

FOR THE CAUSE OF LIFE

If you faint in the day of adversity,
your strength is small.
Rescue those who are being taken away to death;
hold back those who are stumbling to the slaughter.
If you say, "Behold, we did not know this"...
Does not He who keeps watch over your soul know it,
and will He not requite man according to his work?

PROVERBS 24:10-12

O Mary, bright dawn of the new world, Mother of the living, to you do we entrust the cause of life: Look down, O Mother, upon the vast numbers of babies not allowed to be born, of the poor whose lives are made difficult, of men and women who are victims of brutal violence, of the elderly and the sick killed by indifference or out of misguided mercy.

Grant that all who believe in your Son may proclaim the Gospel of life with honesty and love to the people of our time. Obtain for them the grace to accept that Gospel as a gift ever new, the joy of celebrating it with gratitude throughout their lives, and the courage to bear witness to it resolutely, in order to build, together with all people of good will, the civilization of truth and love, to the praise and glory of God, the Creator and Lover of Life. [EV n. 105]

X

PRAYERS FOR SPECIAL DAYS
AND SEASONS

Teach us to number our days aright,
that we may gain wisdom of heart.

PSALM 90:12 NAB

IN ADVENT

*I will not leave you desolate; I will come to
you. Yet a little while, and the world will see
Me no more, but you will see Me; because I live,
you will live also ... If a man loves Me, he will
keep My word, and My Father will love him, and
We will come to him and make Our home with him.*

JOHN 14:18, 19, 23

We begin this perpetual, daily adoration of the Blessed
Sacrament at the beginning of Advent ... The Eucharist is
the sacramental testimony of Your first coming, with which
the words of the prophets were reconfirmed and expecta-
tions were fulfilled. You have left us, O Lord, Your Body
and Blood under the species of bread and wine that they
may bear witness to the fact that the world has been
redeemed—that through them Your Paschal Mystery may
reach all men as the sacrament of life and salvation. The
Eucharist is at the same time a constant announcement of

Your second coming and the sign of the definitive Advent and also of the expectation of the whole Church.

"When we eat this bread and drink this cup, we proclaim Your death, Lord Jesus, until You come in glory."

Every day and every hour we wish to adore You, stripped under the species of bread and wine, to renew the hope of the "call to glory",[1] the beginning of which You constituted with Your glorified body "at the Father's right hand".

One day, O Lord, You asked Peter: "Do you love Me?"

You asked him three times—and three times the apostle answered: "Lord, you know everything; You know that I love You."[2]

May the answer of Peter ... be expressed by this daily and day-long adoration which we have begun today.

May the unworthy successor of Peter in the Roman See—and all those who take part in the adoration of Your eucharistic Presence—attest with every visit of theirs and make ring out again the truth contained in the apostle's words:

"Lord, You know everything; You know that I love You." Amen. [OR 12-14-81]

TO THE MOTHER OF ADVENT

Now when these things begin to take place, look up and raise your heads, because your redemption is drawing near.

LUKE 21:28

AT ADVENT

O Mother of our Advent,
be with us and see to it
that He will remain with us
in this difficult Advent
of the struggles for truth and hope,
for justice and peace:
He, alone, Emmanuel! [OR 1-7-80]

AT CHRISTMAS

May Christmas find each of us
engaged in rediscovering the message
that comes from the manger in Bethlehem.
A little courage is necessary,
but it is worthwhile,
because only if we can open out in this way
to the coming of Christ
will we be able to experience
the peace announced by the angels
during that holy night.
May Christmas be for you all
a meeting with Christ,
who became man to give every man
the capacity of becoming a son of God.   [OR 1-4-82]

TO EMMANUEL, "GOD WITH US"

*B*ehold, an angel of the Lord appeared to him in a dream, saying, "Joseph, son of David, do not fear to take Mary your wife, for that which is conceived in her is of the Holy Spirit; she will bear a son, and you shall call His name Jesus, for He will save His people from their sins." All this took place to fulfil what the Lord had spoken by the prophet:

"Behold, a virgin shall conceive and bear a son, and His name shall be called Emmanuel" (which means, God with us).

MATTHEW 1:20-23

Emmanuel! You are in our midst. *You are with us.* Coming down to the uttermost consequences of that Covenant made from the beginning with man, and in spite of the fact that it was violated and broken so many times...

You are with us! *Emmanuel!*

In a way that really surpasses everything that man could have thought of You. You are with us as *Man*.

You are wonderful, truly wonderful, O God, Creator and Lord of the Universe, God with the Father Almighty! The Logos! The only Son!

God of power! You are with us as man, as a newborn baby of the human race, absolutely weak, wrapped in swaddling clothes and placed in a manger, "because there was no place for them" in any inn.[3]

Wonderful! Messenger of Great Counsel!

Is it not precisely because You became man in this way, came into the world in this way, without a roof to shelter You, that You became nearest to man?

Is it not precisely because You Yourself, the newborn Jesus, are without a roof that You are nearest to those brothers and sisters of ours ... who have lost their homes ... ? And the people who really come to their aid are precisely the ones who have You in their hearts, You who were born at Bethlehem without a home.

Is it not precisely because from the first days of Your life, You were threatened with death at the hands of Herod that You are particularly close, the closest, to those who are threatened in any way, those who die at the hands of murderers, those who are denied basic human rights?

And still more: Is it not for this reason that You are closer to those whose life is already threatened in their mother's womb?

O truly wonderful! The God of power in His weakness as a Child ... Could You have done anything more than You have done, in order to be Emmanuel, God with us?...

You are the Prince of Peace! Peace: what a great good it is for people! How much it is desired in the modern world, and at the same time, how much it is threatened.

You are *Father forever*. Man, who grows from his many-sided past, faces the future, and at the same time worries about his own future, about the future of the world. Christ, may You be the future of man!

Isaiah said that upon Your shoulders "dominion rests".[4] What is this dominion upon Your shoulders, weak Child, what is this dominion?

We know what it is. You have enabled us to know it completely, from the manger to the cross, from Bethlehem to Calvary, from Your birth to Your resurrection.

It is not dominion "over man". It is dominion "for man". It is the power of the redemption. It is truth and love.

Behold, You are born in Bethlehem, that in You may be revealed that love with which the Father has so loved the world as to give His only-begotten Son ...[5]

"A Child is born to us, a Son is given to us." Yes! A Son has been given to us. In this Son we are all once more given back to ourselves! He is our blessing. [OR 12-29-80, 1]

"THE WORD BECAME FLESH"

In the beginning was the Word, and the Word was with God, and the Word was God … In Him was life, and the life was the light of men. The light shines in the darkness, and the darkness has not overcome it … And the Word became flesh and dwelt among us, full of grace and truth; we have beheld His glory, glory as of the only Son from the Father.

JOHN 1:1, 4, 5, 14

"The Word became flesh and dwelt among us."[6]
Let us welcome Him.

Let us, too, say: Behold, I have come to do your will.[7] Let us be available for the action of the Word, who wishes to save the world also through the collaboration of those who have believed in Him.

Let us welcome Him. And with Him, let us welcome every man. The darkness still seems always to want to prevail: wicked riches, selfish indifference to the sufferings of others, mutual mistrust, hostility between peoples, the hedonism that obscures reason and perverts human dignity, all the sins that offend God and go against love of our neighbour. We must bear witness to faithfulness, though in the midst of so many counter-testimonies. We must be, although among so many non-values, the value of good which overcomes evil with its intrinsic power.

The cross of Christ gives us the strength; Mary's obedience sets us the example. Let us not draw back. Let us not be ashamed of our faith. Let us be stars that shine in the world, light that attracts, warmth that persuades.

[OR 3-30-81, 4, 12]

FOR CHILDREN AT CHRISTMAS

And they went with haste, and found Mary and Joseph, and the babe lying in a manger.

LUKE 2:16

What joy is greater than the joy brought by love?
What joy is greater than the joy which You, O Jesus,
bring at Christmas to people's hearts, and especially to
the hearts of children?

Raise Your tiny hand, divine Child,
and bless these young friends of yours,
bless the children of all the earth.   [TPS 40/3, 1995, 146]

AT YEAR'S END

*The true light, which enlightens everyone,
was coming into the world.
He was in the world,
and the world came to be through Him,
but the world did not know Him.
He came to what was His own,
but His own people did not accept Him.*

*But to those who did accept Him He gave the
power to become children of God, to those who
believe in His name.*

JOHN 1:9-12 NAB

Although we are aware of the coursing waves of evil,
and feel more and more often how that evil threatens man,
his life, his dignity, and his conscience, yet we end this year
too with the "Te Deum" of thanksgiving.

We give thanks once more because the Word "became

flesh and dwelt among us".[8] We give thanks because together with Him, there came into the world the fullness of grace and truth; because we have all received and continually receive from this fullness.

We give thanks even amid the most painful trials, because the light shines continually in the world, even if the darkness has not accepted it. Amen. [OR 1-11-82, 13]

ON NEW YEAR'S DAY

To the King of ages, immortal, invisible, the only God, be honour and glory for ever and ever. Amen.

1 TIMOTHY 1:17

"To Him belong time and the centuries.
To Him be glory and power
for ever and ever."[9]

Besides greeting you, dear brothers and sisters, I greet the new year, above all by glorifying God who alone is eternal, unlimited by time. He alone is Truth and Love. He is Omnipotence and Mercy. He alone is Holy.

He is the One who is.

He is the Father, Son, and Holy Spirit in the absolute Unity of the Divinity. So I greet this new year together with you in the Name of our Lord Jesus Christ: there is, in fact, no other Name in which we could be saved.[10]

In the Name of Jesus Christ I embrace this year, that it may be a time of salvation for the Church and for the world.

In the Name of Jesus Christ I say to this year:
"The Lord bless you and keep you.
The Lord make His face to shine upon you,
and be gracious to you.
The Lord lift up His countenance upon you,
and give you His peace."[11]   [OR 1-11-82, 1]

IN LENT

Search me, O God, and know my heart!
Try me, and know my thoughts!
And see if there be any wicked way in me
and lead me in the way everlasting!

PSALM 139:23-24

Glory to You, O Christ, the Word of God.

Glory to You every day in this blessed period of Lent …

Glory to You, Word of God, who became flesh and manifested Yourself with Your life and carried out Your mission on earth with Your death and resurrection.

Glory to You, Word of God, who penetrate the recesses of human hearts, and show them the way to salvation.

Glory to You in every place on earth …

Glory to You, Word of God, Word of Lent, which is the time of our salvation, of mercy and repentance …

Glory to You, Word of God!   [OR 3-31-80, 6]

ON GOOD FRIDAY

If God is for us, who can be against us? He who did not spare His own Son but handed Him over for us all, how will He not also give us everything else along with Him? . . . It is Christ Jesus who died, rather, was raised, who also is at the right hand of God, who indeed intercedes for us. What will separate us from the love of Christ? Will anguish, or distress, or persecution, or famine, or nakedness, or peril, or the sword? . . . No, in all these things we conquer overwhelmingly through Him who loved us. For I am convinced that neither death, nor life, nor angels, nor principalities, nor present things, nor future things, nor powers, nor height, nor depth, nor any other creature will be able to separate us from the love of God in Christ Jesus our Lord.

ROMANS 8:31-39 NAB

Jesus Christ, we are about to conclude this holy day of Good Friday at the foot of Your cross. Just as once in Jerusalem at the foot of the cross there stood Your Mother, John, Mary Magdalene, and the other women, so do we stand here. We are deeply moved by the importance of the moment. We cannot find the words to express all that our hearts feel. This evening, when—after You had been taken down from the cross, they laid You in a tomb at the foot of Calvary—we wish to ask You to stay with us through Your cross; You, who through the cross took leave of us. We ask You to stay with the Church: to stay with humanity; not to be dismayed if many, perhaps, pass by Your cross with indifference, if some go away from it, and others do not reach it.

And yet, perhaps, never so much as today has man had need of this power and this wisdom that You Yourself are, You alone: through Your cross!

So stay with us in this deep mystery of Your death, in which You revealed how much "God loved the world".[12] Stay with us and draw us to Yourself;[13] You who fell beneath this cross. Stay with us through Your Mother, to whom from the cross, You especially entrusted every human being.[14]

Stay with us!

Stat Crux, dum volvitur orbis! Yes, "the Cross stands high upon the world as it goes around!"   [OR 4-17-79, 11]

AT THE EASTER VIGIL

If Christ has not been raised, your faith is futile and you are still in your sins. Then those also who have fallen asleep in Christ have perished. If for this life only we have hoped in Christ, we are of all men most to be pitied.

But in fact Christ has been raised from the dead, the first fruits of those who have fallen asleep. For as by a man came death, by a man has come also the resurrection of the dead. For as in Adam all die, so also in Christ shall all be made alive.

1 CORINTHIANS 15:17-22

Christ, Son of the living God!

Here we are, Your Church; the body from Your Body and from Your Blood; here we are, keeping watch …

We keep watch, in order to precede those women, who "at early dawn" will go to the tomb, "taking the spices which they had prepared" with them,[15] to anoint Your body placed in the tomb on … Friday.

We keep watch, in order to be near Your tomb, before Peter comes here, brought by the words of the three women, before Peter comes, who, stooping, will see only the linen cloths; and he will return to the apostles "wondering at what had happened".[16]

What had happened was what the women had heard: Mary Magdalene and Joanna and Mary the Mother of James, when they had arrived at the tomb and had found the stone rolled away from the tomb, "but when they went in there did not find the body" of the Lord Jesus. At that moment, for the first time in that empty tomb in which Your body was laid the day before yesterday, there rang out the words: "He is risen!"[17]

"Why do you seek the living among the dead? He is not here, but has risen. Remember how He told you, while He was still in Galilee, that the Son of Man must be delivered into the hands of sinful men, and be crucified, and on the third day rise."[18]

For this reason we are here now. For this reason we are keeping watch. We wish to precede the women and the apostles. We wish to be here, when the sacred Liturgy of this night will make present Your victory over death. We wish to be with You, we, Your Church, the Body from Your Body and from Your blood shed on the cross …

There are many of us keeping watch at Your tomb this night. We are all united by "one faith, one Baptism, one God and Father of us all".[19] We are united by the hope of resurrection, which springs from the union of life, in which we wish to remain with Jesus Christ.

We rejoice in this holy night together with those who have received Baptism here. It is the same joy that the disciples and confessors of Christ have lived during the night of the resurrection in the course of so many generations. The joy of the catechumens on whom the water of Baptism was poured, and the grace of union with Christ in His death and resurrection.

It is the joy of life that we share with one another in the night of the resurrection as the deepest mystery of our hearts, and we wish it to everyone ...

Christ, the Son of the living God, accept from us this holy vigil on Easter night ... You, our paschal Lamb!

[OR 4-14-80, 12]

AN EASTER BLESSING

If then you have been raised with Christ, seek the things that are above, where Christ is, seated at the right hand of God ... Let the word of Christ dwell in you richly ... as you sing psalms and hymns and spiritual songs with thankfulness in your hearts to God. And whatever you do, in word or deed, do everything in the name of the Lord Jesus, giving thanks to God the Father through Him.

COLOSSIANS 3:1, 16-17

May the joy of the risen Christ always fill your hearts!
May Easter make you understand more and more that the whole of life must be a song of goodness and innocence, by means of the grace that Jesus has earned for us with His passion, death, and resurrection! [OR 5-4-81, 9]

TO CHRIST ON EASTER MORNING

When the perishable puts on the imperishable, and the mortal puts on immortality, then shall come to pass the saying that is written:

"Death is swallowed up in victory.
O death, where is thy victory?
O death, where is thy sting?"

The sting of death is sin, and the power of sin is the law. But thanks be to God, who gives us the victory through our Lord Jesus Christ.

Therefore, my beloved brethren, be steadfast, immovable, always abounding in the work of the Lord, knowing that in the Lord your labour is not in vain.

1 CORINTHIANS 15:54-58

Paschal Victim! You know all the names of evil better than anyone else is able to name or list them. You embrace all the victims of evil!

Paschal Victim! Crucified Lamb! Redeemer! *Agnus redemit oves.*

Even if in the history of man, individuals, families, society, and indeed all of humanity evil has developed disproportionately, eclipsing the horizon of good, nonetheless, it will not overcome You!

Death will no longer strike You!

The risen Christ will never die again.

Even if in the history of man—and in the time in which we live—evil would increase its power; even if humanly speaking one could not envision the return of social love to the world, [the return to a] world in which people live in peace and justice,

—even if humanly one could not see [such a] passage,

—even if the powers of darkness and the forces of evil would rage, You, Paschal Victim! Lamb without spot! Redeemer! You have already obtained the victory! *Your Easter is the passage!*

You have already obtained the victory!

And You have made it *our victory!* The paschal meaning of the life of Your people.

Agnus redemit oves.

Christus innocens Patri reconciliavit peccatores.

Evil will never be reconciled with good.

But people, *sinners,* the people struck by evil—and at times profoundly steeped in evil—*Christ has reconciled them with the Father.*

Let us celebrate today the resurrection!

Let us celebrate today the reconciliation!

[OR 4-19-82, 1]

ON PENTECOST

All these with one accord devoted themselves to prayer, together with the women and Mary the Mother of Jesus, and with His brothers ... When the day of Pentecost had come, they were all together in one place. And suddenly a sound came from heaven like the rush of a mighty wind, and it filled all the house where they were sitting. And there appeared to them tongues as of fire, distributed and resting on each of them. And they were all filled with the Holy Spirit and began to speak in other tongues, as the Spirit gave them utterance.

ACTS 1:14, 2:1-4

Let us thank the Holy Spirit for the day of Pentecost! Let us thank Him for the birth of the Church! Let us thank Him because at that birth was present the Mother of Christ, who persevered in prayer with the first community!

Let us give thanks for the motherhood of Mary, which was communicated to the Church and continues to be so! Let us give thanks for the Mother who is ever present in the Upper Room of Pentecost!

Let us give thanks because we can also call her the Mother of the Church!

You, who more than any other human being were entrusted to the Holy Spirit, help your Son's Church to persevere in the same dedication, that she may be able to pour out upon all people the indescribable benefits of redemption and sanctification, for the setting free of the whole creation.[20]

You, who were with the Church at the beginning of her mission, intercede for her, that as she goes into all the world she may continually teach all nations and proclaim the Gospel to every creature. May the word of divine truth and the Spirit of love find entry into people's hearts, because without this truth and this love, they cannot really live the fullness of life.

You, who in the fullest way knew the power of the Holy Spirit, when it was granted to you to conceive in your virginal womb the eternal Word and bring Him into the world, obtain for the Church the gift of being able continually to bring forth through water and the Holy Spirit the sons and daughters of the whole human family, without any distinction of language, race, and culture, thus giving them the "power to become the children of God ..."[21]

You who serve as the Mother of the whole family of the children of God, obtain for the Church that, being enriched by the Holy Spirit with the fullness of the hierarchical and charismatic gift, she may go on with constancy toward the future along the path of that renewal that comes from what the Holy Spirit says ...

God the Holy Spirit! who with the Father and the Son are adored and glorified! Accept these words of humble dedication addressed to You in the heart of Mary of Nazareth, your Spouse and the Mother of the Redeemer, whom the Church too calls Mother, for since the Upper Room of Pentecost the Church learns from her her own vocation as a mother! Accept these words of the pilgrim Church, uttered amid labours and joys, amid fears and hopes, words that are the expression of humble and trusting dedication, words with which the Church [that] was entrusted to You—the Spirit of the Father and the Son—in the Upper Room at Pentecost for ever, does not cease to repeat together with You to [the Church's] divine Spouse: Come! The Spirit and the Bride say to the Lord Jesus, "Come!"[22]   [OR 6-15-81, 10]

ON THE FEAST OF CORPUS CHRISTI

The cup of blessing which we bless, is it not a participation in the blood of Christ? The bread which we break, is it not a participation in the body of Christ? Because there is one bread, we who are many are one body, for we all partake of the one bread.

1 CORINTHIANS 10:16-17

"I am the living bread come down out of heaven."[23] Towards this Bread, dearest brothers and sisters, our hearts turn today with particular intensity of faith and love. To man, a pilgrim on the streets of time, but driven by an insuppressible desire for immortality, Christ comes with His divine food: "He who eats this Bread will live for ever."[24]

Aware of this immense gift, believers wish at least once a year to carry their Lord in triumph: there is no community of Catholics which, on the Solemnity of Corpus Christi, does not come together with joyful adoration around the sacrament of the altar, to bring It with hymns and prayers into the sphere of life and daily work.

We too turn today, with a heart full of gratitude, to Jesus hidden under the veils of bread and wine, and to Him we repeat with the Church: "Good Shepherd, true Bread, O Jesus, have mercy on us. Nourish and defend us, bring us to eternal happiness in the land of the living."[25]

In this act of faith and adoration she is near us who for nine months held under her heart the divine Word made flesh for our salvation. May the holy Virgin enable all of us to welcome the Eucharistic Jesus into our life with the attitude of humble availability and confident abandonment with which she uttered her fiat, which returned to throw open the heavens, making hope blossom once more on the earth.   [OR 6-29-81, 1]

XI

PRAYERS FOR THOSE
WHO HAVE DIED

It is therefore a holy and wholesome thought to pray for the dead, that they may be loosed from sins.

2 MACCABEES 12:45 DR

PRAYER IN A CEMETERY

or now we see in a mirror dimly, but then face to face. Now I know in part; then I shall understand fully, even as I have been fully understood.

1 CORINTHIANS 13:12

The eight Beatitudes are the Gospel code of holiness, by which all those whom the Church remembers today with such veneration and love were inspired and to which they remained faithful up to the end.

For our brothers and sisters who rest in this … cemetery and in all the graveyards of … the world, may the words of Christ in the Sermon on the Mount become the Good News of eternal salvation.

May the kingdom of heaven be theirs.

May they possess it as a "Promised Land".

May they have eternal joy.

May they be satisfied in their hunger and thirst for righteousness.

May they be called children of God forever.

May they see God face-to-face.

May their joy and happiness be full and unlimited.

Let us pray: O God, the glory of believers and the life of the just, who saved us by the death and resurrection of Your Son, be merciful to our deceased brothers and sisters. When they were in our midst they professed faith in the resurrection; give them endless bliss. Through Christ our Lord.   [OR 11-9-81, 2]

FOR MISSIONARIES OF THE PAST

And I heard a voice from heaven saying, "Write this: Blessed are the dead who die in the Lord henceforth." "Blessed indeed," says the Spirit, "that they may rest from their labours, for their deeds follow them!"

REVELATION 14:13

Kneeling in this cemetery at the tomb of the missionaries come from afar, we pray to You, Lord.

Blessed be You, Lord, for the testimony of Your missionaries! It was You who inspired their apostolic hearts to leave forever their land, their family, their native country, to come to this country, unknown to them until then, and to propose the Gospel to those whom they already considered brothers.

Blessed be You, Lord, for having supported their faith and their hope, at sowing time; and throughout their apostolic labour; for having given them resistance and patience in toil, difficulties, sorrows, and sufferings of every kind.

Blessed are You, Lord, for having strengthened their

attachment and trust to the sons of this people, to the extent of considering them, very soon, capable of the life of the baptized and opening to them the way to religious life, to priestly preparation, with the tenacious will of founding, with them and for them, a local Church, the fruits of which we are gathering.

Blessed be You, Lord, for all the graces that have come through their word, through their hands, through their example.

They dedicated their lives to the end for the mission, and they left their mortal remains to this land; some after a life shortened by work, some even after a life risked and offered as martyrs for the faith. The grain of wheat had to fall into the earth and die in order to yield much fruit.

Lord, bring it about that the Church watered by their sweat and their blood may reach its full maturity. Thanks to them, others can harvest today in joy what they sowed in tears. May large numbers come forth among the sons and daughters of this country, to take over from them, in order that Your name may be glorified ...

Let us take care not to forget these pioneers of the Gospel, in the memory of the heart and of prayer. We hope that You have welcomed them into Your paradise, forgiving the weaknesses that may have marked their lives like those of all human beings. Give them the reward of good and faithful servants. May they enter the joy of their Master. Give them eternal rest and may Your light shine upon them forever. Amen.   [OR 5-26-80, 10]

FOR A DECEASED FRIEND

Even though I walk through the valley of the
shadow of death, I fear no evil;
for thou art with me; thy rod and thy staff,
they comfort me.
Thou preparest a table before me in the presence
of my enemies;
thou anointest my head with oil, my cup overflows.
Surely goodness and mercy shall follow me all the
days of my life;
and I shall dwell in the house of the Lord forever.

PSALM 23:4-6

Let us bow our heads before the inscrutable plans of
God, just as [he] bowed his head when, advised by his
doctors, he knew the end was near.

At that moment, emotions similar to those expressed in
the Psalm ... certainly flooded into his heart:

"The Lord is my light and my salvation;
whom should I fear?
The Lord is my life's refuge;
of whom should I be afraid? ...
One thing I ask of the Lord;
this I seek:
To dwell in the house of the Lord
all the days of my life,
that I may gaze on the loveliness of the Lord ...
I believe that I shall see the bounty of the Lord
in the land of the living!"[1]
We trust that he has reached that "land".

And if some residue of human weakness should still prevent that full "seeing the bounty of the Lord" which was the aspiration of his whole life, today we raise our prayer for his soul that the moment of the ultimate and beatifying encounter with God may be hastened.

May he sit at that table where, according to the striking image of the ... Gospel, the "master of the house" himself "will put on an apron ... and proceed to wait on" the guests:[2] that is, the table where the soul's food will be the vision of God Himself, who with the wealth of His love will be the inexhaustible fount of an eternal joy without shadow. Amen! [OR 11-22-82, 4]

BESIDE THE COFFIN OF A CARDINAL

When we cry, "Abba! Father!" it is the Spirit Himself bearing witness with our spirit that we are children of God, and if children, then heirs, heirs of God and fellow heirs with Christ, provided we suffer with Him in order that we may also be glorified with Him.

ROMANS 8:15-17

Death is always man's last experience, and it is inescapable. A difficult experience, before which the human soul feels fear. Did not Christ Himself say: "Now is my soul troubled. And what shall I say, 'Father, save me from this hour'?" [And He added at once:] "No, for this purpose I have come to this hour. Father, glorify Thy name."[3]

Father, glorify!

There remains that last cry of the soul, in such contrast with the experience of death, with the experience of the destruction of the body, in which "the whole creation has been groaning in travail together until now"!⁴ Yet, groaning and suffering the pains of death, it does not cease to wait "with eager longing for the revealing of the sons of God".⁵ And we know "that the sufferings of this present time are not worth comparing with the glory that is to be revealed in us".⁶

Let us too, then, before this coffin, in the spirit of that special communion that united us, give expression to these desires:

Father, forgive! Father, absolve! Father, purify! Purify in the measure of the holiness of Your face.

And finally: Father, glorify!

With all humility, but at the same time with all the realism of our faith and hope, let us raise this prayer beside the coffin of our brother.   [OR 3-26-79, 11]

PRAYERS TO THE
BLESSED VIRGIN MARY

And a great portent appeared in heaven, a woman clothed with the sun, with the moon under her feet, and on her head a crown of twelve stars ... She brought forth a male Child, one who is to rule all the nations with a rod of iron.

REVELATION 12:1, 5

TO THE MOTHER OF GRACES

And Mary said, "Behold, I am the hand-maid of the Lord; let it be to me according to your word."

LUKE 1:38

I greet you, Mother of Graces! ... When I proclaim Christ, the Son of the living God, "God from God", "Light from Light", "of the same substance as the Father",[1] at that moment I profess with the whole Church that He became man through the Holy Spirit and was born of the Virgin Mary. Your name, Mary, is indissolubly connected with His Name. Your call and your "yes" belong inseparably, therefore, from that moment onwards, to the mystery of the Incarnation.

With the whole Church I profess and proclaim that Jesus Christ in this mystery is the only mediator between God and man: for His incarnation brought to Adam's sons, who are subjected to the power of sin and death, redemption and justification. At the same time, I am deeply convinced [that] no one has been called to participate so deeply as you, the Mother of the Redeemer, in this immense and extraordinary mystery. And no one is better able than you alone, Mary, to let us penetrate this mystery more easily and clearly—we who announce it and form a part of it. [OR 12-22-80, 12]

TO THE IMMACULATE ONE,
FULL OF GRACE

*And Mary said,
"My soul magnifies the Lord, and my
spirit rejoices in God my Saviour,
for He has regarded the low estate of His hand-
maiden.
For behold, henceforth all generations will call me
blessed;
for He who is mighty has done great things for
me, and holy is His name.*

LUKE 1:46-49

Mary, you said under the inspiration of the Holy Spirit that the generations would call you blessed. We take up again the song of past generations so that it will not be interrupted, and exalt in you the most radiant being that mankind has offered to God: the human creature in its

178

perfection, created anew in justice and holiness in a peerless beauty which we call "the Immaculate" or "Full of Grace".

Mother, you are the "New Eve". The Church of your Son—aware of the fact that only with "new men" is it possible to evangelize, namely, to bring the "Good News" to the world to make a "new humanity"—[the Church] beseeches you that through your intercession the newness of the Gospel, the seed of holiness and fruitfulness, may never be lacking among men.

Mary, we worship the Father because of the prerogatives that shine in you, but we worship Him also because you are always for us "the handmaid of the Lord", a little creature. Because you were capable of saying *"Fiat"* ["Let it be"], you became the Bride of the Holy Spirit and the Mother of the Son of God.

Mother who appears in the pages of the Gospel showing Christ to the Shepherds and the Wise Men, ensure that every evangelizer—bishop, priest, man and woman religious, father or mother, youth or child—be possessed by Christ in order to be capable of revealing Him to others.

Mary, hidden in the multitude while your Son works the miraculous signs of the birth of the Kingdom of God, and who speaks only to tell others to do whatever He says,[2] help evangelizers to preach not themselves, but Jesus Christ.

Mother, wrapped in the mystery of your Son, often without being able to understand, but capable of storing everything and pondering it in your heart,[3] bring it about that we evangelizers shall always understand that beyond techniques and strategies, preparation and plans, to evangelize is to immerse oneself in the mystery of Christ and to try to communicate something of Him to one's brothers.

Our Lady of genuine humility, who taught us in the prophetic canticle that "God always exalts the humble",[4] always helps "the simple and the poor" who seek you with their ordinary piety; help the pastors to lead them in the light of truth and at the same time to be strong and understanding when they have to uproot certain elements that are no longer genuine, and purify certain expressions of popular devotion. Amen.   [OR 8-11-80, 4]

TO THE DAWN OF SALVATION

But when the fullness of time had come, God sent His Son, born of a woman ... so that we might receive adoption.

GALATIANS 4:4-5 NAB

O shining Virgin, hope and dawn of salvation for the whole world, turn your kind, maternal look upon us all, gathered here to celebrate and proclaim your glories!

O faithful Virgin, you who have always been ready and quick to receive, preserve, and meditate upon the Word of God, also make us, amid the tragic events of history, know how to maintain always intact our Christian faith, a precious treasure handed down to us by the Fathers!

O powerful Virgin, who with your feet crushes the head of the tempting serpent, make us fulfil, day after day, our baptismal promises by which we renounced Satan, his works, and his allurements, and let us know how to give the world a joyful witness of Christian hope.

O merciful Virgin, who has always opened your maternal heart to the call of humanity, at times divided by indifference and even, unfortunately, by hatred and war, make us all know how to grow always, according to the teaching of your Son, in unity and peace, in order to be worthy children of the only heavenly Father. Amen. [OR 9-29-80]

"DO WHATEVER HE TELLS YOU"

Then His mother and His brothers came to Him but were unable to join Him because of the crowd. He was told, "Your mother and Your brothers are standing outside and they wish to see You." He said to them in reply, "My mother and My brothers are those who hear the word of God and act on it."

LUKE 8:19-21 NAB

Mother ... at this solemn moment we listen with particular attention to your words: "Do whatever my Son tells you."[5] And we wish to respond to your words with all our heart. We wish to do what your Son tells us, for He has the words of eternal life. We wish to carry out and fulfil all that comes from Him, all that is contained in the Good News, as our forefathers did for many centuries.

Their fidelity to Christ and to His Church, and their heroic attachment to the Apostolic See, have in a way stamped on all of us an indelible mark that we all share. Their fidelity has, over the centuries, borne fruit in Christian heroism and in a virtuous tradition of living in accordance with God's law, especially in accordance with the holiest commandment of the Gospel—the commandment of love. We have received this splendid heritage from their hands at the beginning of a new age, as we approach the close of the second millennium since the Son of God was born of you, our *alma mater;* and we intend to carry this heritage into the future with the same fidelity with which our forefathers bore witness to it ...

May our ears constantly hear with the proper clarity your motherly voice: "Do whatever my Son tells you." Enable us to persevere with Christ. Enable us, Mother of the Church, to build up His Mystical Body by living with the life that He alone can grant us from His fullness, which is both divine and human. [OR 10-8-79, 14]

MOTHER OF CONSOLATION

But standing by the cross of Jesus [was] His mother ... When Jesus saw His mother, and the disciple whom He loved standing near, He said to His mother, "Woman, behold your son!" Then He said to the disciple, "Behold your mother!" And from that hour the disciple took her to his own home.

JOHN 19:25-27

The Blessed Virgin continues to be the loving consoler of humanity in the many physical and moral sufferings that afflict and torment it. She knows our sorrows and our griefs, because she too suffered from Bethlehem to Calvary: "and a sword will pierce through your own soul too".[6] Mary is our spiritual Mother, and a mother always understands her own children and consoles them in their troubles.

She had, moreover, from Jesus on the cross that specific mission to love us, and only and always to love us in order to save us! Mary consoles us above all by pointing out to us Christ crucified, and paradise.

O Blessed Virgin, be the one and perennial consolation of the Church that you love and protect! Console your bishops and your priests, missionaries, and religious, who must illumine and save modern society, which is difficult and sometimes hostile! Console Christian communities, giving them the gift of numerous, strong, priestly and religious vocations!

Console all those who are invested with authority and civil and religious responsibilities, so that we may have as our goal, always and only, the common good and man's complete development, in spite of difficulties and defeats!

Console ... the many families of migrants, the unemployed, the suffering, those who bear in their body and soul the wounds caused by dramatic situations of emergency; the young, especially those who, for so many tragic reasons, are confused and disheartened; all those who feel in their hearts an ardent need of love, altruism, charity, and dedication, who cultivate high ideals of spiritual and social conquests!

O consoling Mother, console us all, and make everyone understand that the secret of happiness lies in goodness, and in always following faithfully your Son, Jesus.

[OR 4-28-80, 4]

TO THE IMMACULATE HEART

And His father and His mother marvelled at what was said about Him; and Simeon blessed them and said to Mary His Mother,

"Behold, this Child is set for the fall and rising of many in Israel,

and for a sign that is spoken against

(and a sword will pierce through your own soul also),

that thoughts out of many hearts may be revealed."

LUKE 2:33-35

O Immaculate Heart! Help us to conquer the menace of evil, which so easily takes root in the hearts of the people of today, and whose immeasurable effects already weigh down upon our modern world and seem to block the paths towards the future!

From famine and war, deliver us.

From nuclear war, from incalculable self-destruction, from every kind of war, deliver us.

From sins against the life of man from its very beginning, deliver us.

From hatred and from the demeaning of the dignity of the children of God, deliver us.

From every kind of injustice in the life of society, both national and international, deliver us.

From readiness to trample on the commandments of God, deliver us.

From attempts to stifle in human hearts the very truth of God, deliver us.

From sins against the Holy Spirit, deliver us, deliver us.

Accept, O Mother of Christ, this cry laden with the sufferings of all individual human beings, laden with the suffering of whole societies.

Let there be revealed once more, in the history of the world, your infinite power of merciful love. May it put a stop to evil. May it transform consciences. May your Immaculate Heart reveal for all the light of Hope.

[OR 5-24-82, 13]

XIII

PRAYERS TO THE SAINTS
AND WITH THE SAINTS

Therefore, since we are surrounded by so great a cloud of witnesses, let us also lay aside every weight, and sin which clings so closely, and let us run with perseverance the race that is set before us, looking to Jesus the pioneer and perfecter of our faith.

HEBREWS 12:1-2

ON THE FEAST OF SAINT JOSEPH

Look kindly on the prayer and petition of your servant, O Lord ... Listen to the petitions of your servant and of your people.

1 KINGS 8:28, 30 NAB

Let us raise together our prayer to God, through the intercession of Saint Joseph, the head of the Holy Family of Nazareth and patron saint of the universal Church.

Let us pray together and say: Lord, hear us!

For all the pastors and ministers of the Church, that they may serve the People of God with active and generous dedication, as Saint Joseph served the Lord Jesus and His Virgin Mother in a worthy way, Lord hear us!

For the public authorities, that in the service of the common good they may direct economic and social life with justice and uprightness, in respect for the rights and dignity of all, Lord, hear us!

That God may deign to unite with the passion of His Son the toil and suffering of the workers, the anguish of the unemployed, the grief of the oppressed, and that He may give help and comfort to everyone, Lord, hear us!

For all our families and for all their members: parents, children, the old, relatives, that, in respect for the life and personality of each one, they may all collaborate in the growth of faith and charity, to be real witnesses of the Gospel, Lord, hear us!

O Lord, bestow on Your faithful the Spirit of truth and peace, that they may know You with all their soul, and generously carrying out what pleases You, may always enjoy Your benefits.

Through Christ our Lord. Amen.   [OR 3-24-80, 12]

TO SAINT JOSEPH OUR TEACHER

Hear, O sons, a father's instruction,
and be attentive, that you may gain insight;
for I give you good precepts;
do not forsake my teaching.

PROVERBS 4:1-2

May Saint Joseph become for all of us an exceptional teacher in the service of Christ's saving mission, a mission which is the responsibility of each and every member of the Church: husbands and wives, parents, those who live by the work of their hands or by any other kind of work, those called to the contemplative life, and those called to the apostolate.

This just man, who bore within himself the entire heritage of the Old Covenant, was also brought into the beginning of the New and Eternal Covenant in Jesus Christ. May he show us the paths of this saving Covenant as we stand at the threshold of the next millennium, in

which there must be a continuation and further development of the "fullness of time"[1] that belongs to the ineffable
mystery of the Incarnation of the Word.

May Saint Joseph obtain for the Church and for the
world, as well as for each of us, the blessing of the Father,
Son, and Holy Spirit.   [RC n. 32]

TO THE APOSTLES PETER AND PAUL

You are fellow citizens with the saints and members of the household of God, built upon the foundation of the apostles and prophets, Christ Jesus Himself being the cornerstone, in whom the whole structure is joined together and grows into a holy temple in the Lord; in whom you also are built into it for a dwelling place of God in the Spirit.

EPHESIANS 2:19-22

Blessed are you, Paul of Tarsus, the apostle of the Gentiles, the converted persecutor, the admirable lover and witness of the crucified and risen Christ! Blessed are you, the apostle of Rome, rooted together with Peter in the very beginning of the Church in this capital. Blessed are you, steward of the mysteries of God—you, for whom "to live is Christ";[2] you, who desire so much and so exclusively to be called the minister of Christ—and who desire to be only that—so that your and our Master speaks in you. She, whom the Father chose to be the Mother of His eternal Son, also speaks in the same way. She was the first to say of herself: "Behold, I am the handmaid of the Lord!"[3]

We bless you Paul and Peter, on the day of your joint feast, and we thank God because before this city—and before the world—you became such great witnesses to the truth, according to which "the Word became flesh and dwelt among us ..."[4]

May I, following you, Peter, proclaim everywhere Christ, who is the Son of the living God and who alone has "the words of eternal life".[5]

May I, following you, Paul, repeat: Let no one think of us differently from what we are, namely, "servants of Christ and stewards of the mysteries of God".[6]   [OR 7-7-80, 2]

TO SAINT TERESA OF JESUS,
A "FRIEND OF GOD"

You are my friends if you do what I command you. No longer do I call you servants, for the servant does not know what his master is doing; but I have called you friends, for all that I have heard from My Father I have made known to you.

JOHN 15:14-15

May the ardent prayer of the pilgrim Pope now ascend to the Father through your intercession, Teresa of Jesus.

I pray for the Church, our Mother: "May this bark of the Church not be always in so great a storm."[7]

Intercede for its evangelizing expansion and for its holiness, for its pastors, theologians, and ministers, for the men and women consecrated to Christ, for the faithful of the family of God.

I pray for a world at peace, without fratricidal wars such

as those that wounded your heart.

Reveal to all Christians the interior world of the soul, a hidden treasure within us, a luminous castle of God. Make the exterior world preserve the imprint of the Creator, and may it be an open book that speaks to us of God.[8]

Receive my supplication for the souls which praise God in tranquillity, for those who have received the great dignity of being friends of God, for those who search for God in the darkness, that they may have revealed to them the light which is Christ.

Bless those who strive for understanding and harmony, those who promote brotherhood and solidarity, because "it is necessary to support one another" and "charity grows when it is communicated".[9]

Protect seafarers and those who work on the land, those who labour and those who make work available; watch over old people, who find in you a model of wisdom and of untiring creativity.

Bless families, the young, and children. May they find a world of peace and liberty, one worthy of people called to communion with God, where they will be able to develop those human virtues which you brought to the splendour of Christian holiness: truth, justice, fortitude, and respect for persons, joy and affability, sympathy and gratitude.

I place in your hands the cause of the poor, whom you so loved.

Bring to fulfilment your ideals of justice in a fraternal communion of goods. All possessions come from God, and

He distributes them to some who are administrators for Him, so that they will share them with the poor.[10]

Intercede for the sick, for whom you cared until the end of your life. Help the destitute, those on the fringe of society, the oppressed, so that in them the dwelling of God, His image and likeness, will be respected and honoured.

Teresa of Jesus! ... To you who are a friend of God and of mankind, whose writings are straight paths to unity, I commend the unity of the Church and of the human family: among Christians of different confessions, among members of different religions, among peoples of different cultures. May all think of themselves as you thought of them: "sons of God and brothers ..."[11]

Teresa of Jesus, hear my prayer! May this thanksgiving of the Church ascend to the throne of the Wisdom of God, for what you have been and for what you still are among the People of God which honours you as doctor and spiritual teacher. [OR 11-29-82, 7]

TO SAINT STANISLAUS, PATRON OF POLAND

Behold, I have taught you statutes and ordinances, as the Lord my God commanded me ... Keep them and do them; for that will be your wisdom and your understanding in the sight of the peoples, who, when they hear all these statutes, will say, "Surely this great nation is a wise and understanding people."

DEUTERONOMY 4:5, 6

Saint Stanislaus, our patron, the protector of the whole country, help us, teach us to be victorious, teach us to attain victory from day to day. Patron of the moral order of our country, show us how we must attain it, by carrying out the work of indispensable renewal, which begins in man, in every man, which embraces the whole of society and all the dimensions of its life: spiritual, cultural, social, and economic ... Teach us this ... and help us to attain this victory in our generation. Amen.   [OR 5-18-81]

TO SAINTS CYRIL AND METHODIUS

Go therefore and make disciples of all nations, baptizing them in the name of the Father and of the Son and of the Holy Spirit, teaching them to observe all that I have commanded you; and lo, I am with you always, to the close of the age.

MATTHEW 28:19-20

O Saints Cyril and Methodius, who brought the faith with admirable dedication to peoples thirsty for the truth and the light, let the whole Church always proclaim the crucified and the risen Christ, the Redeemer of Man!

O Saints Cyril and Methodius, who in your hard and difficult missionary apostolate always remained deeply bound to the Church of Constantinople and to the Roman See of Peter, bring it about that the two sister Churches, the Catholic Church and the Orthodox, having overcome the elements of division in charity and truth, may soon reach the full union desired!

O Saints Cyril and Methodius, who with the sincere spirit of brotherhood approached different peoples to bring to all the message of universal love preached by Christ, bring it about that the peoples of the European continent, aware of their common Christian heritage, may live in mutual respect for just rights and in solidarity, and be peacemakers among all the nations of the world!

O Saints Cyril and Methodius, who, driven by love for Christ, abandoned everything to serve the Gospel, protect the Church of God: me, Peter's successor in the Roman See; the bishops, priests, men and women religious, men and women missionaries, fathers, mothers, young men, young women, the poor, the sick and the suffering; may each of us, in the place in which Divine Providence has placed us, be a worthy "labourer" of the Lord's harvest! Amen!   [OR 3-16-81]

AT THE TOMB OF SAINT ALBERT THE GREAT

Who is wise and understanding among you? By his good life let him show his works in the meekness of wisdom ... The wisdom from above is first pure, then peaceable, gentle, open to reason, full of mercy and good fruits, without uncertainty or insincerity.

JAMES 3:13, 17

God, Thou art wondrous in Thy saints!

Appointed by You to the highest office of the Church of Jesus Christ, I kneel today as a pilgrim at the tomb of Saint Albert, to glorify You with all the faithful ... and to thank You for his life and works, through which You gave him to the Church as a teacher of the faith and an example of Christian life.

God, our Creator, cause and light of the human spirit, You gave Saint Albert a profound knowledge of faith in true imitation of our Lord and Master Jesus Christ. The world itself became for him the revelation of Your omnipotence and goodness.

Through his contact with Your creation he learned to recognize and love You more profoundly. At the same time he researched through the works of human wisdom, including the writings of non-Christian philosophers, and paved the way for their encounter with Your Gospel.

Through the gift of discrimination You made him uniquely able to avoid error, to establish truth more deeply and make it known among men. In doing so You made him a teacher of the Church and of all mankind.

With the intercession of Saint Albert we pray together to You for Your mercy:

— Send to Your Church teachers of truth in our time as well, who will be capable of interpreting and preaching Your Gospel to the people of the world through their words and saintly living. Hear us, O Lord.

— Open the hearts of men through the grace of a living faith so that they may recognize God's presence in His creation and their own lives and come to correspond more and more perfectly with His holy will.

— Accompany and illuminate the work of scientists and scholars with Your Holy Spirit. Preserve them from pride and self-conceit and give them a sense of responsibility in their dealings with the gifts of Your creation.

— Give those responsible in state and society insight and responsibility so that they may use the achievements of science and technology for peace and progress among the peoples of the world and not for their harm or destruction.

— Help us all to recognize the truth amidst the many dangers and errors of our time and to serve You devoutly in a life strengthened by faith ...

Pray for us, Saint Albert, that we may be made worthy of the promises of Christ.

Let us pray: God, our refuge and strength, You gave the saintly bishop and teacher of the Church, Albert, the power to associate human knowledge with eternal wisdom. With his intercession, strengthen and protect our faith in the intellectual confusion of our days. Give us the openness of his intellect so that the progress of science may also help us to know You more profoundly and come closer to You. Let us grow in the knowledge of the truth which You Yourself are so that we may one day see You face-to-face in the presence of all the saints. For this we pray through Christ our Lord. Amen.   [OR 11-24-80, 3]

TO SAINT FRANCIS OF ASSISI

And the King will answer them, "Truly, I say to you, as you did it to one of the least of these My brethren, you did it to Me."

MATTHEW 25:40

Help us, Saint Francis of Assisi, to bring Christ closer to the Church and to the world of today. You who bore in your heart the vicissitudes of your contemporaries, help us, with our heart close to the Redeemer's heart, to embrace the lives of the people of our time. The difficult social, economic, and political problems, the problems of culture and contemporary civilization, all the sufferings of the people today, their doubts, their denials, their disorders, their tensions, their complexes, their worries …

Help us to express all this in the simple and faithful language of the Gospel. Help us to solve everything on an evangelical level, in order that Christ Himself may be "the Way, the Truth, and the Life" for the people of our time.[12]

This is asked of you, holy son of the Church, son of the Italian land, by Pope John Paul II, son of Poland. And he hopes that you will not refuse him, that you will help him. You have always been kind and you have always hastened to bring help to all those who appealed to you. [OR 11-16-78]

TO THE BLESSEDS

Strive for peace with all men, and for the holiness without which no one will see the Lord.

HEBREWS 12:14

Full of deeply felt joy we thank God who continues to bestow bountifully the gift of holiness, and we bow reverently to venerate the new Blesseds ... Let us listen docilely to the message they address to us by the power of their witness ... On this day of glory they remind us that we are all invited and bound to pursue the holiness and perfection of our own state ... and that the Church, which lives in time, is missionary by her very nature and must follow the same path followed by Christ—that is, the way of poverty, obedience, service, and self-sacrifice until death ...

O Blesseds, whom the pilgrim Church glorifies and exalts today, give us the strength to imitate your limpid faith, when we find ourselves in moments of darkness; your serene hope, when we are disheartened by difficulties; your ardent love of God, when we are tempted to idolize creatures; your delicate love of brothers, when we would like to shut ourselves up in our selfish individualism!

O Blesseds, bless your countries, those of your origin, and those given to you by God, like the "Promised Land" to Abraham, and which you loved, evangelized, and sanctified!

O Blesseds, bless the whole Church, a pilgrim that is awaiting her lasting country!

O Blesseds, bless the world, which is hungry and thirsty for holiness! ...

Pray for us! [OR 6-30-80, 11]

A FINAL PRAYER

Jesus said . . . "Abide with Me and I in you . . . for apart from Me you can do nothing."

JOHN 15:4, 5

I leave you now with this prayer that the Lord Jesus will reveal Himself to each one of you, that He will give you the strength to go out and profess that you are Christian, that He will show you that He alone can fill your hearts. Accept His freedom and embrace His truth, and be messengers of the certainty that you have been truly liberated through the death and resurrection of the Lord Jesus. This will be the new experience, the powerful experience, that will generate, through you, a more just society and a better world.

God bless you, and may the joy of Jesus be always with you! [OR 11-5-79, 2]

NOTES

Meditations on Prayer

1. Galatians 4:6.
2. Luke 11:1.
3. St. Augustine, *Confessions*, I, 1.
4. See Luke 18:1.
5. See Psalm 139:14.
6. See Genesis 1:27; Psalm 8:5.
7. John 17:11, 14.
8. See Hebrews 5:7.
9. Luke 11:13.
10. Romans 8:26.
11. Romans 8:27.
12. See Matthew 6:9.
13. See Luke 11:13.
14. 1 Peter 2:5.
15. Matthew 18:19-20.
16. Romans 8:26.
17. John 15:5.
18. See Acts 1:13-14.
19. See Acts 1:8.

I
Prayers to God the Father

1. Luke 1:50 RSV.
2. Matthew 5:7 RSV.
3. Luke 23:34.
4. Matthew 27:46.
5. Luke 23:46.

II
Prayers to God the Son

1. John 12:31.
2. See Luke 23:46.
3. Romans 6:5.
4. See Luke 24:29.
5. See Revelation 21:3.

III
Prayers to God the Holy Spirit

1. Sequence for Pentecost.
2. See John 16:22.
3. See Romans 14:17; Galatians 5:22.
4. John 14:17.
5. See Isaiah 11:2.
6. See Ephesians 2:2; 6:12; 1 John 4:1-6.
7. See Ephesians 4:30.
8. See 1 John 3:19.
9. See Romans 12:2.
10. See 1 Corinthians 13:4-7.

IV
Prayers for the Church

1. John 17:21.
2. *Didache* 10, 5.
3. See Matthew 18:20.
4. John 17:21.
5. See Mark 10:27.
6. See Isaiah 25:9.
7. From the Byzantine Liturgy.
8. Ephesians 4:30.
9. Matthew 28:19.
10. See 2 Corinthians 6:1.
11. See Luke 1:50.
12. Luke 1:38.
13. 2 Peter 3:13.
14. 1 Corinthians 1:24.
15. John 2:5.
16. See Matthew 9:38; Luke 10:2.
17. John 4:35-36.
18. See John 4:15.
19. See Matthew 9:37.
20. See John 8:12.
21. Ephesians 2:4.
22. See Ephesians 2:10.
23. Ephesians 1:12.
24. Litany of the Sacred Heart; see 1 John 2:2; Ephesians 2:14; Romans 3:25; 5:11.
25. Pope John Paul II, General Audience Address of January 4, 1984: *Insegnamenti,* VII, 1 (1984), 16-18.
26. *Insegnamenti,* VII, 1 (1984), 16-18.
27. See Galatians 4:4.
28. See John 17:21-23.

V

Prayers for the Family

1. See Ephesians 3:15.
2. The Roman Missal, Preface of Christ the King.
3. Ephesians 3:15.

VI

Prayers for Groups with Special Concerns

1. See 1 Corinthians 12:4ff.
2. See Luke 2:52.
3. Mark 16:15.
4. John 1:4.
5. John 20:21.
6. See Matthew 5:9.
7. Matthew 25:40.
8. John 15:1.
9. Matthew 5:13.
10. Matthew 5:3.
11. Matthew 6:19-20.
12. See Genesis 12:2ff.
13. See Psalm 122:6-9.

VII

Prayers for Peace

1. Matthew 6:13.
2. Matthew 5:9.

X
Prayers for Special Days and Seasons

1. See 1 Peter 5:10.
2. See John 21:15-17.
3. Luke 2:7.
4. See Isaiah 9:5.
5. See John 3:16.
6. John 1:14.
7. See Hebrews 10:7, 9.
8. John 1:14.
9. Liturgy of Holy Saturday.
10. See Acts 4:12.
11. See Numbers 6:24-26.
12. See John 3:16.
13. See John 13:32.
14. See John 19:27.
15. See Luke 24:1.
16. See Luke 24:12.
17. See Luke 24:3, 5.
18. See Luke 24:5-7.
19. See Ephesians 4:5-6.
20. See Romans 8:21.
21. John 1:12.
22. See Revelation 22:17.
23. See John 6:51.
24. See John 6:58.
25. Sequence.

XI
Prayers for Those Who Have Died

1. See Psalm 27 [26]:1, 4, 13.

2. See Luke 12:37.
3. John 12:27.
4. Romans 8:22.
5. Romans 8:19.
6. Romans 8:18.

XII
Prayers to the Blessed Virgin Mary

1. From the Nicene Creed.
2. See John 2:5.
3. See Luke 2:19, 51.
4. See Luke 1:52.
5. See John 2:5.
6. See Luke 2:35.

XIII
Prayers to the Saints and with the Saints

1. See Galatians 4:4.
2. Philippians 1:21.
3. See Luke 1:38.
4. John 1:14.
5. John 6:68.
6. 1 Corinthians 4:1.
7. St. Teresa of Avila, *The Way of Perfection*, 35, 5.
8. See St. Teresa, *Life*, 9, 5.
9. *Life*, 7, 22.
10. See St. Teresa, *Thoughts on the Love of God*, 2, 8.
11. St. Teresa, *The Interior Castle*, V. 2. 11.
12. John 14:6.